First and Last Love

First and Last Love

Thoughts and Memories About Music

Robert W. Miles

SUNSTONE PRESS

SANTA FE

Sunstone books may be purchased for educational, business, or sales promotional use.
For information please write: Special Markets Department, Sunstone Press,
P.O. Box 2321, Santa Fe, New Mexico 87504-2321.

Book and Cover design › Vicki Ahl
Body typeface › Goudy Old Style
Printed on acid-free paper
∞
eBook 978-1-61139-252-4

Library of Congress Cataloging-in-Publication Data

Miles, Robert W., 1920-, author.
   First and last love : thoughts and memories about music / by Robert W. Miles.
      pages cm
   ISBN 978-0-86534-268-2 (softcover : alk. paper)
   1. Miles, Robert W., 1920- 2. Lyricists--United States--Biography. 3. Warren,
Chandler. I. Title.
   ML429.M536A3 2013
   780.92--dc23
   [B]
                                            2013046100

WWW.SUNSTONEPRESS.COM
SUNSTONE PRESS / POST OFFICE BOX 2321 / SANTA FE, NM 87504-2321 /USA
(505) 988-4418 / ORDERS ONLY (800) 243-5644 / FAX (505) 988-1025

To my late wife, Jeanne

Contents

Preface

The narrative in this autobiography emanates from the subtitle, "Thoughts and Memories about Music." In some chapters thought predominates, in others, memory. In most chapters the two are intertwined.

The earliest memory related is that of a four-year-old Bobby Miles in 1924 sitting in his sandbox in Auburn, Alabama, listening to and memorizing the tunes of college songs being sung by students passing by. The last memory in the book is that of the author receiving in mid-2013 a song lyric to which he hopes to write music.

To be sure, there is a kind of back and forth movement. Chapter 2, "Art vs. Commerce," is mainly an expression of long-held thoughts with a number of musical memories to substantiate them; while chapter 3, "Mandatory Opinions," is, despite its title, a memory the author hopes never to forget.

"My Timing Was All Wrong," chapter 4, sounds as though it is going to be a litany of "reasons" for not "making it big" as a songwriter. Actually, it is a well-documented historical essay combining both thoughts and memories.

The fact that the author, though musically inclined, had to live with no piano in the house until he was in his mid-twenties, combined with the fact that in order to write the many song melodies that were going through his head, he had to have a rudimentary knowledge of the keyboard account for the inclusion of several chapters about the piano. Some, like "The Rudiments of Jazz Piano Improvisation," are mainly thoughtful. Others, like "From Upright to Baby Grand," in which the piano gets stuck in the stairwell between the first and second floors of an apartment house, are mainly memories.

In the book as a whole most of the thoughts are important to the author, while most of the memories are happy ones.

Foreword

I come to praise Bob Miles a/k/a Robert W. Miles. After all, he is the composer of the vast majority of songs I have written. I consider myself very lucky to have had this experience.

Working with Bob since 1955, we have created eleven children's "musicals, a musical revue of our songs and three full-length Broadway style musicals. Plus many, many standalone songs. I can't remember even a single time when voices were raised in anger, tempers flared or selfishness of any kind has marred our working or our personal relationship. I have been blessed.

We've worked together in every way possible. Bob calls me to say he has a new melody. I call him about or send him a new lyric. We meet for hours, where I relentlessly press Bob to play the song again and again until I can find the words that I believe belong to the tune.

Bob is a consummate musician, and I am in awe of his talent. Although we've never had a shot at Broadway, I know our work has the quality to succeed there. And so, as many theatre people say: it's one-half talent and one-half luck. Also, I believe it's the era into which one is born. Bob and I got together just as the traditional Broadway musical was coming to an end. I sincerely believe it will return to what it was, because almost all of today's new musicals are not good. And that's not because there aren't good writers, but the current thinking is that the old way is passé. Yet you can see that it is the revivals of the old musicals that dominate successful shows on Broadway and on the road.

Bob and I have had our share of success because there have been any number of talented singers who sing our songs in their acts and on recordings. We've had productions of a number of our musicals across the United States. And we've had a hell of a lot of fun (and work) in writing them all.

You can't ask for more than that. And you could never have a writing partner more talented, more gracious, more understanding, more patient and more wonderful than Bob Miles.

Thank you, Bob.

—Chandler Warren

Santa Fe, New Mexico

September 2013

1

Singing in My Sandbox

The first music I remember consciously listening to was a college song sung by students of the Auburn Polytechnic Institute in the small town of Auburn, Alabama, in 1924. I was four years old. Sitting in my front yard sandbox I would first hear the song in the distance being sung by two or three undergraduates on their way to the school. The song would reach a crescendo as these students trod the unpaved "sidewalk" a few yards from my sandbox, then gradually fade away as they got nearer to their destination. When I could hear them no longer I would hum the tune over and over. I would then get out of the sandbox and toddle back and forth, still humming it.

In 1926 our family moved to Lynchburg, Virginia, when my father became minister of the Westminster Presbyterian Church there. By that time I had moved on from humming the songs I heard to actually singing them. One of the popular songs of 1926 was "Gimme a Little Kiss, Will Ya, Huh?" (and I'll Give it Right Back to You). After hearing me singing to myself up and down the church corridors before and after Sunday School, one of the church leaders saw to it that I was cast in a church community room play in which I propelled myself across the stage in a toy roadster, pulled up beside one of the little Sunday School girls and sang the song. After the song I would get out of the roadster, put my arms around her and kiss her. This, as you can well imagine, brought down the house.

In 1929 I spent happy summer evenings under our green and white striped porch awning listening to a radio from across the street. Our family was to get its first radio in 1933. One song played over and over in the summer of 1929 was "The Wedding of the Painted Doll." It made a lasting impression on me. A few years later, when it became important to me to learn who wrote the songs I was listening to, I learned that these engaging words were by Arthur Freed and the catchy music by Nacio Herb Brown. This and other songs by this composer, such as "You are my Lucky Star" and "Singing in the Rain," have the simplicity of genius. For example, what songwriter has ever made better use of the musical interval of the octave?

In 1935 my family and I visited relatives in New York. For tourists like us a visit to Radio City, and most especially the two-year-old Radio City Music Hall, was mandatory. The movie showing while we were there was *Top Hat* with Fred Astaire and Ginger Rogers. Because of a traffic tie-up on the way to the theater we were being ushered into center mezzanine seats a few minutes after the film had started, just when Fred Astaire and Ginger Rogers found themselves caught in the rain in a London park pavilion and the initial strains of the song "Isn't This a Lovely Day to Be Caught in the Rain" were being played.

There is no way to describe the effect this had on a very susceptible fifteen-year-old on his first visit to New York. The brilliant score proceeded through the songs "Top Hat," "Cheek to Cheek" and culminated in "The Piccolino." I remained transfixed when the movie ended and from the depths of the auditorium there arose a pipe organ from which an accomplished musician sent this brilliant and deathless score echoing from the gilded heavens of the theater. Then legions of men in black tights, sombreros, and cummerbunds and equally brilliantly dressed women appeared on the side balconies of the theater singing the infectious "Piccolino."

Here I will say parenthetically that, much as I loved the whole score of *Top Hat*, "Isn't This a Lovely Day?" remained my favorite song from it. I think this may be an early example of my penchant for long melodic lines in songs.

When the movie started again I was intensely aware of the credits, most especially, "Lyrics and Music by Irving Berlin." "Mother," I asked, "Who is Irving Berlin?" My mother said she had "grown up on Irving Berlin." She told me that his real name was Israel Belin, that he had married New York socialite Ellen Mackey and that during the depression Ellen Mackey's father, Clarence Mackey, the tycoon, had found it necessary to borrow money from Irving Berlin, the little Jewish boy he had not wanted his daughter to marry.

I thought all of this was interesting; in fact I could not learn enough about Mr. Berlin. It had suddenly become a magic name, and it has always remained so. But at that time my admiration for him was all tied up with my admiration for the movie *Top Hat*. When we returned to Kentucky from our New York visit, I saw it again. That fall I entered Darlington Preparatory School in Rome, Georgia. When *Top Hat* came to that city, I saw it again.

The next summer while back in Lexington for vacation from prep school, I was still preoccupied with it. I knew all of the songs by heart, of course, and sang them over and over. I had come to identify with Fred Astaire and would spend hours trying to dance like him. I also tried to walk like him and talk like him. It was one thing to practice all of this in front of a big mirror in my own room. But at Saturday night country club dances I would use my dancing partner as a kind of prop around whom I would try ever more elaborate steps and movements. The word soon got around among Lexington high school girls: "Watch out for Bobby Miles."

I have never questioned the appropriateness nor the validity of my reaction that summer night in 1935 when I walked into Radio City Music Hall and heard the music of *Top Hat* for the first time. Each subsequent time I have seen the movie, I have been able to understand why it was an apocalyptic experience for me. The wonder of a work of art always remains.

I have heard Irving Berlin criticized for having so often written about dancing or the weather. It is true, there are many such songs, but what wonderful songs they are. There is such craftsmanship, such beauty, such honest sentiment as opposed to sentimentality. In popular songs, style and manner are as important as content.

To be sure, I was now beginning to focus on this content as expressed in the lyrics of songs. Thus my love and admiration for the songs of Irving Berlin continued to grow as I saw the movies *Follow the Fleet* in 1936, *On the Avenue* in 1937, and *Carefree* in 1938.

And my obsession with Fred Astaire took me to all of his movies many times. One of these was *Shall We Dance?* that introduced me to the Gershwins, or, rather, made me really focus on them for the first time. I had *heard* "Rhapsody in Blue" a few years earlier while visiting my cousin in Reading, Massachusetts. The guy in the apartment below was trying to learn how to play it. In addition to *Shall We Dance?* I loved the Gershwins' score for *A Damsel in Distress* just as much.

During this period I also saw the movie *Swing Time* with its score by Jerome Kern, music, and Dorothy Fields, lyrics. Kern became in my mind part of that great triumvirate—Gershwin, Kern, and Irving Berlin. When I began writing songs ten years later, it was the music of Kern that I studied most and with which I felt the most affinity.

2

Art vs. Commerce

t was a happy circumstance that my love for the songs of Irving Berlin, George and Ira Gershwin, and Jerome Kern was enhanced by listening to great recordings of their work by the band of clarinetist Artie Shaw. As an eighteen-year-old Fred Astaire in 1938, I was naturally also drawn to the bands of Benny Goodman and Tommy Dorsey. But there was something very special musically about Artie Shaw's band. In addition to the famous recording of Cole Porter's song "Begin the Beguine," there was a string of outstanding songs superlatively arranged for orchestra by Shaw himself and by Jerry Gray—such songs as the Gershwins' "The Man I Love" and "Oh, Lady be Good," Irving Berlin's "Supper Time" and Kern's "All the Things You Are" and "Bill." In addition there were wonderful Shaw original compositions like "Any Old Time," "The Back Bay Shuffle," and "I'm in Love with the Honorable Mr. So and So."

And the Shaw band featured one of the best vocalists the popular music world has ever had—Helen Forrest. Her greatness was exemplified by the fact that she did not interpose herself between the song and the listener. Her mission was to serve the song in the clearest, most effective way. And the same was true of the Shaw orchestra's big band arrangements. They expressed fully the music inherent in the song.

There were, of course, many performances and recordings by bands and vocalists in the late nineteen thirties until the mid-nineteen forties in which the fullest expression of the song, both musically and lyrically, was the primary concern. To cite only three such examples, one was drummer Gene Krupa's song "Drumboogie," with a vocal by Anita O'Day; another was the Count Basie orchestra's interpretation of the great song "Time on my Hands," with music by Vincent Youmans and lyrics by Harold Adamson and Mack Gordon; and a third was the Benny Goodman orchestra's performance of the great Cole Porter song "Ev'ry Time We Say Goodbye."

One should not make sweeping, all-knowing pronouncements, but it does seem evident that the period of the late nineteen thirties to the mid-nineteen forties was one of the last times that art and commerce coalesced. Earlier periods would have to include the entire writing careers of Irving Berlin, George and Ira Gershwin, and Jerome Kern. And examples abound in the other popular arts—the motion picture *Wuthering Heights*, to name only one.

Art and commerce *should* coalesce, if only to get the artist paid what he or she deserves. People who are misguided enough to distrust all commercialism might have a hard time appreciating the *artistry* of Berlin, Kern, the Gershwins, or Artie Shaw. They were artists first, and the fact that they were well paid for their efforts was a happy result of a total giving of themselves to their art. Their impulses and motivation were, I feel sure, mainly artistic, not commercial. Nor, incidentally, were they commercially competitive. A young Gershwin would stand outside Kern's window and listen for inspiration, not to copy what he heard. And Kern said of Berlin: "Irving Berlin has no place in American music. He *is* American music."

It is the commercial habit of mind that should be eschewed. The commercial habit of mind in the nature of the case makes criticism impossible—criticism in its negative function of identifying the meretricious—criticism in its positive function of seeing and acknowledging the excellent, the priceless, and explaining what this excellence consists of and how it is achieved.

The commercial habit of mind as it functions in relation to popular music is interested only in what sells, regardless of its musical or lyrical value. Looking again at the big band era we must acknowledge that many of the recordings were cynical commercial exploitations of a few *riffs* that had *made it*, and that many of the songs performed and recorded were second or third rate.

In a well-written song the lyric and the music are of equal importance. But in the mid to late nineteen forties and early nineteen fifties lyrics came to predominate in *novelty* songs, such as "Mairzy Doats" and "How Much is that Doggie in the Window?"—harmless but meaningless. Songs as such became less popular than dance rhythms like disco or singers like Elvis Presley.

I am tempted to say that that part of the listening public whose musical taste had been questionable to begin with, preferring as they did the bands of Guy Lombardo and Sammy Kaye to those of Benny Goodman and Artie Shaw, were in a few years to have what little taste they had bludgeoned to death by the relentless and egomaniacal beat of rock and disco.

A kinder way of putting it is that the subject matter of popular songs expanded exponentially beyond romantic love and came to include many, if not all, aspects of life and experience. Traditional melodies, lyrics, and dance rhythms were not enough to express all of this.

3

Mandatory Opinions

*T*he thoughts and feelings expressed in the previous chapter always summon up the memory of an experience I had at the very time I was formulating them. In the late nineteen thirties, when I was still a teenager and still living in Kentucky, I remember thinking that if a person were intelligent about one thing, he or she would be intelligent about other things; or, more precisely, if he or she were intelligent and sensitive about one of the arts, this would carry over into the other arts, making the person intelligent and sensitive about them also. I was about to learn that this is not always true, especially when it comes to music.

My mother had a good friend whose daughter, a woman about ten years older than I, had gone to New York some years earlier and had achieved some success as a writer on the staff of a national magazine. My mother also did some writing, and her friend's daughter in New York, whose name was Catherine, had arranged for a literary agent for my mother. Catherine and my mother corresponded pretty regularly, and once in a while Catherine would come to Lexington for a visit with *her* mother. When that happened, the two of them would always come for a visit at our house. I was very much in awe of Catherine, the New York writer.

At about this time, as I have written earlier, I was becoming excited by the music of clarinetist and bandleader Artie Shaw. It was more than just teenager enthusiasm for a popular big band I could jitterbug to. I had been studying music for a few years and was playing violin in the University of Kentucky symphony orchestra. That didn't necessarily qualify me as an authority on swing music, but I was able to hear something very special in Artie Shaw, and I was very responsive to his music. I would listen to his records over and over again for hours, finding them musically inexhaustible, as much so as any piece of perfectly constructed classical music.

I felt a strong need to communicate this enthusiasm to somebody, somebody who knew about these things, somebody professional. I was sure my mother was tired of hearing me rave about Artie Shaw. I don't mean to be unkind when I say that I wasn't sure she knew what I was talking about anyway. "Why don't you write to Catherine?" asked Mother. "I'm sure she would be most interested in your opinions. It would also give you practice in setting your thoughts down on paper."

This idea appealed to me very much, so I wrote a very long letter to Catherine, explaining in the greatest detail what it was I liked so much about Artie Shaw. I assumed that she was as familiar with all his records as I was and that she would agree when I said things like, "Although 'The Man I Love' is a greater song and his recording of it is superb it just might be that 'Lover Come Back to Me' has a slight edge on it. In both recordings the saxophones weaving around the melody and becoming ever more convoluted are without parallel anywhere; but there's a little more intensity, a little more musical build-up in 'Lover Come Back to Me.' It may be the greatest record he has made."

After mailing this letter, I could hardly wait for Catherine's response, expressing her enthusiastic agreement, saying how perceptive I am about music and how well I write about it.

Before very long, Catherine did answer my letter, saying, "Dear Bobby,

Your comments about Artie Shaw were interesting, but here in New York we like Guy Lombardo."

Not "I like Guy Lombardo" but "we" do, giving it more authority.

"Here in New York"—the only opinion that matters. Being liked in New York makes it official and mandatory. The supposition is that the few can speak for the many. If there are people who don't think Guy Lombardo is the best in popular music, they just don't know what they are expected to think.

None of this, of course, has anything to do with critical standards or sound musical judgment. Guy Lombardo's music, while pleasant and suitable for middle-aged couples to dance to, was very far removed aesthetically from that of Artie Shaw.

This experience with Catherine has been repeated from time to time through the years when I have found that people with good sense about and good taste in one art can be less than perceptive about another.

4

My Timing Was All Wrong

I began writing songs in 1946. Although it is unbecoming of a songwriter to attribute his only modest success to causes other than his own limitations, I wish to point out that in the years after World War II, the general public's interest in the well-written popular song underwent a noticeable decline.

There were a number of reasons for this. For one thing, the country was experiencing a kind of cultural awakening. The development of the long-playing record brought with it not only the classical music repertory but also many releases of superb prewar popular recordings. And increasingly improved fidelity began to foster an interest in, even a preoccupation with, sound for its own sake.

These developments were heartening, and it would be churlish to minimize their importance. Nevertheless, they just might have militated against the writing and appreciation of the first-rate popular song. The seasoned listener can usually take in his stride both a symphony and a song. But the person who has for the first time in his life been staggered by the complex musical wonder of a Beethoven symphony and who is beginning to realize how much more there is to hear might be inclined to regard a new, well-written popular song as a good deal less important.

The development of high fidelity and the widespread appreciation of the classical repertory, then, did not serve the songwriter well. But they were a great help to the orchestral arranger, who for many years had been the forgotten man of popular music. For the arranger the song is only the starting point, or thematic subject matter for a more extended musical composition; and good arrangements—those by Nelson Riddle or Billy May, for example—had the kind of structural coherence found in classical works. Moreover, improved fidelity enlarged the spectrum of sound available to the arranger, making it possible for men like Andre Kostelanetz and Percy Faith to use such symphonic colors as large string choirs and French horns to stunning advantage.

But welcome as these developments were, they might very well have worked against the writing of really good new songs. For one thing, there was the very large catalog of outstanding songs by Irving Berlin, Jerome Kern, George Gershwin, Cole Porter, Richard Rodgers, Vincent Youmans, and Harold Arlen, which cried aloud to be given new arrangements and played on new high fidelity equipment. And the improved fidelity coincided with a widespread cultural nostalgia at this time. Books about the nineteen twenties and thirties sold in the millions, and old movies were a staple of popular culture. So it was with old songs. People felt the need to revisit the more stable world in which these songs were written.

That said, most records after the war were bought for their overall sound. The art of orchestral arranging had become an end in itself, and every arranger had his own style, his own sound, which he imposed on all material that came his way. This had always been true to some extent, but in the years before the war the emphasis was on arranging a certain song in the way most appropriate for that song. All the big dance bands of the nineteen thirties had their distinctive sound, which was given to them by their arrangers, but there was as much interest in the song itself as in the arrangement—Eddie Sauter's arrangement of "The Man I Love" for the

Benny Goodman Orchestra is a classic arrangement of that song that brings out all of its inherent beauty in a definitive way. Many arrangements for the other big bands, especially Artie Shaw's, served the song in the same way.

With the shift in emphasis after the war from what was recorded to how it was recorded, it became all too evident that a good orchestral arrangement can make anything sound good. Faced with the necessity of filling both sides of a long-playing record, the record companies and arrangers not only gave too much of a sound-alike quality to many of the great "standard" songs of the past but also gave the same orchestral treatment to countless second and third rate songs. The reductio-ad-absurdum of these lowered standards was the music piped into waiting rooms, bars, and restaurants—music that had a pervasive wall-to-wall sound. People seemed to welcome having music all around them all the time more than ever before, but, paradoxically, were less discriminating than ever before about what they listened to. Perhaps it would be more accurate to say that their musical taste and standards were being lowered daily without their knowing it.

If the orchestral arranger came into his own after the war, the singer did so equally, if not more so. Here again the emphasis shifted from what was performed, the song, to how it was performed and by whom. When we think of singers before, or during, the war, we think of them in relation to certain songs—Judy Garland singing "Over the Rainbow" or Bing Crosby singing "White Christmas." After the war, we came to think of Frank Sinatra and Perry Como as singers and personalities more than as singers of any particular song. There were good reasons for this. With so much demand for long-playing records and so much new talent getting into the act, a singer had not only to develop a very strong individual style but also to sell himself or herself by projecting his or her personality. So it was that the cult of personality, always strong in American life, became even more pronounced.

One of the strongest components of the cultural awakening that manifested itself during the 1950s was jazz music. Jazz concerts were given to sold-out audiences in leading concert halls. Jazz festivals were held all over the country every summer. Academic institutions added jazz to their curricula. Every major record company had its jazz division, and jazz records sold in the millions. Jazz had become respectable.

If interpretation is important in singing, it is everything in jazz. Variation or improvisation on a given melody and progression of chords is the essence of jazz. For the jazz musician the original melody of a song is only the starting point or jumping off place for the creation of new melodies of greater and greater melodic, harmonic, and rhythmic complexity within the framework of a steady beat. At his best, the jazz musician is a composer who erects a musical edifice on the spot rather than thinking it out ahead of time and writing it down. He could be likened to an artist making something out of pliable material. He must work very fast before the material hardens, making sure that when it does it is in the shape he wants it to be.

It is understandable, then, that to the jazz musician and the jazz listener the popular song is important but not preeminent. It is the material he works with, roughly analogous to the folk songs used by some composers of "classical" music as the subject matter for extended works. To be sure, the jazz musician is interested in the better songs, or at least the ones with the most interesting progression of chords; and so he often goes to the old "standards" for his material.

Before the war some of the compositions Duke Ellington wrote for his big band had words written to them and became "standard" songs, sung and recorded by singers and other bands. These include "Mood Indigo," 1931, with words by "Barney" Bigard and Irving Mills; "Solitude," 1934, with words added by Irving Mills and Eddie DeLang; and "Don't Get Around Much Anymore," 1942, with words by Bob Russell.

After the war, however, the jazz-oriented songs that come to mind are instrumentals—"'Round Midnight" and "Ruby, my Dear" by jazz pianist and composer Thelonius Monk. The jazz-influenced songwriters Harold Arlen and Hoagy Carmichael were still writing, but most of their great songs had been written before the war.

During this period, I was in my early thirties, living alone in Manhattan and writing songs that I hoped to get performed. I have exciting memories of going to hear Monk and other great jazz musicians. It was my favorite entertainment.

I have cited a few reasons I believe that first-rate popular songs were not a staple of the postwar years and that, therefore, that era may not have been the most felicitous time to embark on songwriting as a career.

5

Pianoless

There are different kinds of deprivation. I was never hungry, for example, nor deprived of any material necessity; but I was deprived of a piano. I did not fully realize that it was a deprivation until I was nine or ten years old and my family visited relatives in Clearspring, Maryland. In their hall was an old upright piano. I immediately and almost instinctively began picking out tunes on it with one finger. The tunes were those I had heard from the radio across the street while sitting on the front porch of our house in Lynchburg, Virginia. Here at the relatives' piano in Maryland, I was completely transfixed and had to be physically picked up and hauled off to bed.

To be sure, I had been around other pianos from time to time. The one I had seen most often was at my grandfather's home in Roanoke, Virginia, just sixty miles from our home in Lynchburg. But the Roanoke piano was now only a piece of furniture left over from the days years earlier when my mother's brothers and sisters had taken lessons on it. No one could now remember when it had last been used. As I saw it, all that was needed now was to have it moved from Roanoke to Lynchburg and my piano deprivation would have ended. But this was not to be, and in time I would come to understand why.

As a young person, my father had had an unfortunate experience with music. The choir director at the family's church had told him that he would never be able to sing and should forget about it. The effect of this rebuff on him was that from that moment on he was unable to carry a tune, much less sing. Even so, he *was* able to retain a real love and respect for sacred music. Accordingly, the first phonograph record I remember was an old 78 rpm recording of Handel's "Messiah."

For several years now, my parents had had to put up with listening to me singing or whistling the latest *Hit Parade* songs all over the house day and night. If they had agreed to have the old family piano moved from Roanoke, as I now and then quietly requested, it is hard to imagine from their perspective the cacophony they would have had to endure. Therefore, as what they hoped would be an adequate musical substitute, I was given a ten-dollar violin and enrolled in a downtown Lynchburg class where ten or so violin students learned to play in unison such songs of the day as "I Love You Truly." And at home I could close my bedroom door and practice to my heart's content without disturbing my mother and daddy.

Playing the violin did, to some extent, help take my mind off not having a piano on which to pick out tunes I heard from the neighbors' radio, to say nothing of actually learning how to play. After all, the violin is primarily a melodic instrument and so satisfied nicely my penchant for melody. The year was 1930. I was ten years old. The violin was to be my instrument for the next twelve years.

In 1933 we moved from Lynchburg, Virginia, to Lexington, Kentucky. The occasion was my father's becoming the minister of the First Presbyterian Church in that city. Rather than enter another violin class, I began taking private lessons from a very experienced teacher, who was also an orchestral musician. He began to introduce me to good orchestral repertory, a far cry from "I Love You Truly." Two years later I went away to a preparatory school in Rome, Georgia. While there I continued violin lessons at a nearby college.

The prep school students teased me and called me "Rubinoff," the name of a popular radio violinist at that time. I wasn't able to practice in my dormitory room because it would have driven my roommate crazy and provoked further ridicule from other students. So, instead, I made use of a small woodshed at the foot of a hill in back of the school.

One of the students at this southern prep school was a boy from Springfield, Massachusetts, very mature for his age. He, even more than the violin teacher back in Kentucky, furthered my interest in the classical music repertory. In his room he had a recording of Beethoven's "Egmont Overture," which he and I played and analyzed endlessly.

In the summer of 1936 Warner Fletcher invited me to visit his family at their resort home in Marblehead, Massachusetts. From there we all made several visits to Tanglewood, Massachusetts, to hear Serge Koussevitzky conduct the great Boston Symphony Orchestra. At that time the Tanglewood summer music festival was held under an enormous tent. On one of our visits there the program featured Beethoven's Sixth Symphony, the "Pastoral." Just as the orchestra began playing the movement that suggests a storm, our own devastating storm broke out, sending hundreds of us fleeing for safety lest the enormous tent collapse on us. It was not too long after this that Tanglewood installed the large shed, which is still in use.

Classical music, especially that of Beethoven, was becoming more and more important to me. However, love for this music did not in the least lessen my love for popular songs, which I could now listen to in the prep school dormitory. And it was at about this time that I started playing the harmonica, which came to me as naturally as breathing in and out. I found the songs of Stephen Foster especially suitable for this instrument.

My Massachusetts friend, Warner Fletcher, graduated a year ahead of me. Before leaving, he prevailed on me to get some music started in this school. At his urging, I did manage to put together a small orchestra, a glee club, and a music club. The school administration was willing to hire a town violinist to come out to the school and lead the orchestra. It was made up, as I recall, of me on violin and a student each on trumpet, trombone, piano, and drums. We played stock arrangements of current songs, such as "Red Sails in the Sunset."

The glee club was a little larger, having in it a fair number of boys who were willing to try singing. Their repertory was folk and popular. The music club consisted of a few boys who liked to discuss different musical topics and personalities.

Getting these groups started entailed lots of chasing after students to get them to go to rehearsals. It all paid off, however. At the end of the 1937-38 school year, my last one there, the orchestra and glee club gave a radio program on the local Rome, Georgia, station. In the final issue of the school paper that year, one of the faculty members wrote an article entitled, "Miles Places Music on Lakeside Map."

Having now graduated from preparatory school, I returned to my home in Lexington and enrolled at the University of Kentucky, which I attended as a day student. There was, of course, still no piano in the house, but my father now let me use a piano in a Sunday school room at the church that was empty on week days. Here, when I was not attending classes at the university, I would spend hours picking out with one finger songs I had heard in the latest Fred Astaire-Ginger Rogers movie or trying to read the notes, treble and bass, on a piece of sheet music.

As a freshman at the university, I took the required courses and also went back to violin lessons, this time with the head of the university's music department. In the afternoons I worked in the music room lounge of the Student Union Building, playing recordings of classical music for students who had finished attending classes for the day. If there were no students requesting music, I played some for myself. I still adored Beethoven, but I was now becoming transfixed by such works as the Brahms Fourth Symphony and B-Flat Piano Concerto, especially the transcendent passages in the second movement.

By the time I got to be a sophomore, I was proficient enough on the violin to join the university symphony orchestra and occupy the first chair of the second violin section. I still remember hours spent on the opening measures of the Mozart 40th Symphony and months spent learning Beethoven's third symphony, the Eroica. I was now also writing reviews for the university paper of the Sunday afternoon concerts given at the university's Memorial Hall. These concerts were usually by visiting artists, but when the university symphony gave a concert there, I had to play in it and then write as objective a review as I could.

Graduating from the university in June 1942 marked the end of my career as a violinist. Six months later I was drafted into the Army, where I served Stateside until March 1946. On being discharged, I returned to my family home in Lexington and enrolled again at my alma mater, the University of Kentucky, this time to work toward a Masters Degree in English under the "G.I. Bill of Rights." I was now twenty-six.

During my last year in the Army, however, I had kept thinking of original popular song type melodies. Back in Kentucky, I was now inordinately preoccupied with trying to keep several of them in my head until I could learn to write them down and harmonize them. I felt an acute need for music theory lessons and an equally acute need for a piano on which to work these things out. If I had been given to a belief in providence, I would have welcomed what happened next as providential.

An elderly church member was scheduled to enter a nursing home. She had, somehow, to dispose of her old square piano, a Victorian relic. My parents graciously agreed to take it off her hands. In doing so, they were helping her and at the same time helping me. In addition, they were acquiring a very nice, if somewhat unusual, piece of furniture for their living room.

From then on, no matter where I was living, I saw to it that I was never again without a piano of some kind for any appreciable length of time.

6

My First Lyric Co-Writer

Providence was still smiling on me as the saying goes. First I met a music teacher who taught me the rudiments of piano playing. She also helped me transcribe the melodies in my head to music manuscript paper and begin to harmonize them. My problem now was to find a lyric writer. I had to admit that the words I was trying to fit to my melodies were not of the same quality as the music in my tunes. I needed to meet someone who could hear the words inherent in my tunes.

One day, providentially, I was introduced to a local poet, William K. Hubbell. When he expressed some tentative interest in hearing what I had, I sat down at the piano and played one of my melodies for him with one finger, even then stumbling a few times because of the importance of the occasion. Would he like my music?

Hubbell, being a poet and also having seen some movies about songwriters, was able to rise above the circumstance of my limited performance ability and to hear a full orchestra with a large string section playing the melody I had written. When I finished, he stood up and applauded, saying he would be very happy to write with me.

We dived in right away. I would record my melody, still using only one finger. This pianistic limitation could be rationalized as fortuitous in that the melody was clearly delineated, an important consideration when fitting a lyric to it. Bill Hubbell would take the little disc home and play it over and over until he felt he had found the lyric idea inherent in that melody. He would then, he told me, write the lyric in one sitting. The results seemed just right to me. I now wanted to start sending our songs to music publishers. I was convinced that when someone important in the business saw our songs we would be on our way. Hadn't I seen this happen time and again in the movies?

Actually, I was not entirely mistaken. In the summer of 1948, after Bill and I had been writing together about a year and a half, we submitted our country-western type song "Twenty-One Miles from Home" to a nationwide songwriting contest sponsored by an organization called "The Motion Picture Song Contest Association." We had seen it advertised in the Lexington newspaper.

Writing and submitting this song to the contest was the last work Bill Hubbell and I did together in Lexington. In September 1948 I moved to New York. Shortly after settling in there, I got a call from my excited co-writer that we had won the first prize of $1,500. I was excited too, of course, and with my half of what was quite a bit of money in those days, I opened my first New York bank account. But as for the first prize, nothing came of that. No music publisher took it nor did any singer record it. It was to be my experience over and over that nothing ever automatically led to anything else. This could be said to be at least partly my fault. I was never adept at exploiting any advantage I had.

In 1951, now settled in New York but still collaborating with Bill Hubbell long distance, I entered a rhythmic song of ours "Another Day with You" into another nationwide song contest, this one with a New York sponsor. The final judges in this contest were bandleaders Benny Goodman and Duke Ellington and singer Billy Eckstein. Once again, Hubbell and I won first prize, this one being *only* $1,000. After learning we had won, I was told by the sponsors that our song had tied for first place with another song. The sponsors had then called in bandleader Gordon Jenkins to break the tie. Jenkins picked our song.

But once again, nothing ensued. Neither Benny Goodman nor Duke Ellington, Gordon Jenkins nor Billy Eckstein ever used the song, much less recorded it. Nor was it picked up by a music publisher. As before, this was due, to some extent at least, to my lack of enterprise. In musing about this, I would sometimes fall back on an extreme-sounding and maybe unfair explanation: if one has it instilled in him from an early age that material, or worldly, success is of secondary importance to spiritual well-being, that person might subconsciously see to it that he does not become materially successful.

Entering and winning these song contests was almost, but not quite, the end of my collaboration with Bill Hubbell. The local Lexington radio station had put out a call for a new signature theme, words and music. Bill wrote some catchy and appropriate words and sent them to me in New York. I set them to music, a process that was a bit unusual for me because up until now our way of working had been for him to write words to my melodies. The radio station accepted our little ditty and began using it. In the old days back in Lexington everyone had quipped that the call letters "W.L.A.P." stood for "We Let Anybody Play " Perhaps now, in using our signature theme, that was exactly what they were doing.

Not long after this, Bill Hubbell began studies that would culminate in his becoming an Episcopal deacon. And I, busy making a living in New York, would soon be given a music-writing assignment that would entail collaborating with another lyricist. I feel very fortunate to have had William K. Hubbell as my first lyric co-writer, and to this day I cherish, and often sing to myself, some of the many fine songs we wrote together.

Twenty-One Miles From Home
(© 1951)

Verse

I wandered into the county jail
One Sunday afternoon,
And in his cell a cowboy sat
Singing this unhappy tune:

Chorus

This lonesome heart of mine is a-wastin'
So close to my home, boy,
Just twenty-one miles.

My mother's food I seem to be tastin'
Her blueberry pie, boy
Is sweet as her smiles.

I always thought home
Was made just for sleepin'
But now it's keepin'
My very own soul.

So home is where this cowboy is headin'
Just twenty-one miles when
I get my parole.

Another Day With You
(© 1951)

What makes me awake with
The birds in the morning
And sing as I tie my shoe?
Oh, it's not just another day dawning;
It's another day with you.

I smile at the folks that
I pass on the sidewalk
And wave to the clouds in the blue.
Oh, it's not just another good morning;
It's another day with you.

I used to be a lazy guy
Sleeping my life away.
Now there's a darn good reason why
I hurry to start the day.

They tell me that heaven
Has streets gold and pearly,
And possibly this is true.
Oh, but heaven is getting up early
For another day with you.

7

Choosing Songwriting as a Career and Moving to New York

It might be more accurate to say that songwriting chose me. During my last year in the Army, original tunes would come to me unbidden, often when I was walking somewhere. But, of course, most of my time was taken up with military base duties.

When I was discharged in March 1946 and returned to my home in Lexington, the unbidden original tunes became more insistent, prompting me to take piano lessons and spend all my spare time practicing and analyzing music, both classical and popular. But it was still spare time. Most of my time was devoted to working toward a Masters Degree in English at my alma mater, the University of Kentucky. The subject I chose for my thesis was an annotated bibliography of the writings and writings about the Nineteenth Century English poet Samuel Taylor Coleridge. This tied in with my undergraduate work as a philosophy major because Coleridge was also a philosopher.

During this same time, I met an undergraduate senior, Elizabeth Kephart. Less than a year later, she and I were married by my Presbyterian minister father. Through the kindness of a church member, "Pat" and I were able to sublet a small apartment not many blocks from my parents' home. So I now had to say "goodbye" to the old square piano in their living room.

One of the attractions of the sublet apartment we were now moving into was a small upright piano, located in the bedroom of all places. That might have worked for a single person, but not for a newly married couple. Nor would the living room be a suitable place now. Pat needed a desk on which to study her assignments for courses leading up to final exams, and I needed a desk on which to write my 140-page thesis. So we moved the piano into the kitchen. Even with all my studying and thesis writing, I still managed to get in some practicing and to continue studying songs on sheet music, especially those by Jerome Kern. I was also still giving Bill Hubbell, my first co-writer, tunes for which he could write lyrics.

It was now early 1948. In a few months I would get my Masters Degree in English and Pat her B.A. in the same subject. My feeling that I wanted to use the remaining two years of my G.I. Bill of Rights to study music rather than English was becoming stronger. In Lexington, there was an orchestral conductor named Alexander Capurso. As an undergraduate at the university, I had played violin in a college orchestra he was conducting at the time. When I now discussed my feelings with Dr. Capurso, he said, "If you are really serious about studying music full time, you should go to the Julliard School of Music in New York, both for the quality of the instruction there and for the quality of the music you would get to hear in New York." His advice helped to focus my thoughts even more, so that by early summer I had made my decision. It was now mainly a question of getting myself and Pat ready for the move.

I went on a few weeks ahead of her so that I could find a place for us to live and also get enrolled at Julliard. I found very small lodgings on West 82nd Street near West End Avenue. Pat joined me shortly. In my first letter to my parents I wrote, "I hope you are reconciled to my studying music and are not disappointed that I'm not doing something else. I really need about four lifetimes to do everything." A few days later, having enrolled at the school, I wrote them, "I like the atmosphere at Julliard very much. It is liberal and stimulating."

Indeed it was. The courses I signed up for looked very promising, and they turned out to be so. A broad historical survey course called "Literature and Materials of Music" was one Julliard was well-known for at the time. Then there were, of course, "Piano" and "Keyboard Harmony." I was assured that in "Piano" I would be able to continue my study of Bach and Beethoven, composers I had found more to my liking and benefit than Chopin or Liszt. I also signed up for "Orchestration" taught by Henry Brandt. This was a subject I wanted to learn something about even though I did not plan to use it. Then, of course, there was "Composition," which I took every semester while at Julliard. It was taught by an excellent composer named Esther Williamson, later Esther Williamson Ballou. She composed contemporary music and encouraged her students to do so also. Although I was not striving to be a "serious" composer, I loved much contemporary music—that of Stravinsky, Bartok, even Schoenberg and Berg. I was intrigued by what other members of the class wrote. I felt that I learned a lot even in this vicarious kind of way. When my time at Julliard was up, I even took some private lessons with Esther Williamson. Her comment about the little compositions I came up with was, "You'll be rich and famous." Well, not quite, Esther.

By now, Pat and I had moved to a small apartment a few feet below street level on a one-block-long street in lower Manhattan—Stuyvesant Street. Once again, as in Lexington, we inherited an upright piano. The former tenant had moved to a larger apartment into which she would be able to fit a baby grand piano.

Pat and I soon began to live the New York life to the extent we could afford to, which was to a greater extent in 1948 than it would be today. Having grown up in medium-sized Southern towns with their streetcars and busses, I loved the subway and was enjoying the long ride to and from Julliard every day, which at that time was in Morningside Heights, a little north of Columbia University and the Union Theological Seminary. To tell you the truth, I would sometimes on weekends stand in the front of the first car on the subway train and ride it from one end of the line to the other and then back to the station nearest home.

By "living the New York life," Pat and I meant going to English, French. Italian, or German movies or to concerts. Over the years, I have many memories of Carnegie Hall, but one of the first is this. I was standing in the ticket line one day when a man a couple of people ahead of me started speaking to the woman he was with. "You know what they say about musicians?" he asked rhetorically. "The only thing they know is music. They're stupid about everything else." This was in the acoustically live lobby of Carnegie Hall. Probably half the people who heard him were musicians.

A much fonder memory of Carnegie Hall and its lobby was one concert intermission when I was able to introduce Pat to one of my Julliard teachers. Marian Bauer was a well-known musicologist and music critic at the time. She attended many concerts at Carnegie Hall, and though she would not exactly "hold court" in the lobby at intermission, she was often surrounded by many admirers. The class of hers I was in at Julliard was "Literature and Materials of Music."

I had recently written a paper for the class entitled "The Influence of French Impressionism on American Popular Music." Professor Bauer had returned the paper with a note saying it was a very interesting article and one worthy of publication.

8

The Rudiments of Jazz Piano Improvisation

uring my second and final year at Julliard, I continued to take several of the courses I had taken in the first year: notably, "Literature and Materials of Music" and "Composition." Now, however, I was able to add "Jazz Piano Improvisation," something new in the Julliard curriculum. It was not that I expected to become a performing jazz pianist. I had begun studying the instrument much too late for that. But I was sure that in this course I would learn much more about the melodic, harmonic, and rhythmic structure of standard popular songs and in that way become a better songwriter myself.

The instructor, John Mehegan, was a protégé of the great composer and conductor, Leonard Bernstein. Mehegan was not only a fine jazz pianist but was also an innovative musical scholar. During his career he published a number of workbooks on playing jazz piano. The students in his classes had the rare benefit of his analytical thoroughness and creative drive. I had certainly been right in thinking his class would help me in my songwriting.

Just as I had studied privately with the teacher Esther Williamson after taking "Composition" with her at Julliard, I now took lessons with John

Mehegan after leaving the school. By then my wife Pat and I had moved from the below-ground apartment on Stuyvesant Street to a sixth floor walk-up on Thomson Street near Sixth Avenue, still farther south in Manhattan. I still had my small upright piano, which the movers had somehow gotten up the six flights of stairs. The stairs didn't seem to bother John Mehegan either, and I always looked forward keenly to my lessons with him.

Having used up all of my G.I. Bill of Rights, I was now helping to support Pat and me on a very modest-paying "nine-to-five" job. Pat was working also. My songwriting was confined to evenings and weekends, but I was doing quite a bit of it. By now I was transcribing to music manuscript paper not only the melodies I kept thinking of but also the underlying chord progressions and, with a lot of constructive criticism from Mehegan, was making these songs more and more musically interesting.

One of the songs that we worked on together John recorded on the Savoy Records label a few years later, in 1954. It was an "instrumental." That is, it had no words, but John gave it the title "Sirod." His wife at that time was named "Doris." The personnel on this record were John Mehegan, piano; Chuck Wayne, guitar; Vinnie Burke, bass; and Joe Morella, drums. There were other "originals" on the record as well as a few "standards," including "Taking a Chance on Love" and "Stella by Starlight." Reviewing this record for the then-popular trade magazine *Down Beat*, the music critic Nat Hentoff wrote: "'Sirod' is an especially pleasing composition." Considering the company our song was in on this record, that evaluation made me feel especially good. I also took it to be further evidence that writing songs was what I should be doing.

It was while I was studying with him that John Mehegan realized he had more private students than he could comfortably handle and asked me to take some of them, mainly beginners, and especially those living in the outlying boroughs of Brooklyn, the Bronx, and Queens. This, of course, pleased me very much because of the confidence it showed in my ability. In addition, there was a kind of dividend I got from teaching: by focusing on the rudiments of keyboard harmony and simple improvisations on a given melody and progression of chords, I was strengthening my ability as a songwriter. In fact, I even wrote a few songs with one of these students, whose proclivity as a poet was as strong, or stronger, than her musical sense.

But a day of reckoning was at hand. Given the fact that my evenings and weekends were now completely absorbed by both taking and giving lessons in the rudiments of jazz piano improvisation and that, in addition, I was doing more and more songwriting of my own, there was now little time, if any, for "living the New York life" (or any other kind) with Pat. It is understandable then, I suppose, that she became tired of being a struggling songwriter's wife and took up with a man much more practical and down-to-earth than I. It was not many months before she moved out, after which she filed for and was reluctantly granted a divorce.

I was sad, of course, but as I have shown, I had more than enough to occupy me both physically and mentally. And there were additional changes to be dealt with. For one thing, just a short time after Pat moved out, I landed a day job that, though still low paying, would, I felt sure, appeal to me more than any I had had so far. It was as an assistant in the music department of the New York headquarters of the then-important organization, Radio Free Europe, located in midtown Manhattan on West Fifty-Seventh Street near Sixth Avenue. My job was to select and buy American recordings of music that would be broadcast behind the "Iron Curtain."

Now, with only one salary coming in, I needed to find smaller living quarters, preferably ones nearer to my new place of work. And, of course, there was much downsizing to do—much to dispose of in the Thomson Street walk-up apartment, including, unfortunately, my old upright piano. This whole process took almost a year, but by early 1955 I found myself in a rented room (not an apartment) in an elevator-accessible building (not a walk-up) on the southwest corner of Eighth Avenue and West Fifty-Sixth Street, within walking distance of my job at Radio Free Europe.

Walking those long West Fifty-Seventh Street blocks twice a day gave me the comfortable feeling of being where I wanted to be—with Carnegie Hall on one side of the street and the Steinway piano showroom on the other.

9

A Student With Surprises

I didn't mind the long walk up the hill from the end of the subway line in the New York borough of Queens because I got to see all the beautiful homes and flower gardens, each of which seemed more lovely and imaginative than the one before it. Mrs. Shore's house was at the very top of the hill, and, fittingly enough, her garden seemed to crown them all. The first thing she did when I arrived was show it to me proudly, explaining how much loving care had gone into the making of it.

I got so I looked forward to the Monday night music lessons at the Shores. I would be met at the gate by the elegant looking Mrs. Shore and the family's huge and affectionate collie. Inside, the two Shore children would be padding around in their pajamas staying up to hear their mother play. When she shooed them off to bed we would settle down to work, with the collie curled up beside the piano. Midway through the lesson Mr. Shore would come home from a long day at the office, give his wife an affectionate pat and head for the kitchen, where his dinner had been kept warm. This would be the time for a short break with coffee and cake.

Later after the lesson, Mr. Shore would drive me down to the subway station. He was very pleased with the progress his wife was making. He said he had always known she was talented and artistic. She had played the violin as a girl, and during the war, when he was stationed overseas, every letter from her would contain a poem she had just written. Mr. Shore felt that too few women these days develop their talents, and he was glad they had bought the piano and decided on music lessons. He admitted he didn't know much about popular music or jazz piano, but if that's what she wanted he was all for it.

Mrs. Shore was both musical and conscientious. She made such progress with the rudiments of melody, harmony, and keyboard technique that in a very short time I was able to give her a simple improvisation to play. Strictly speaking, of course, improvisation is the spontaneous invention of new melodic ideas around the original melody and chord progressions of a popular song. But at this stage of the game I wanted to show Mrs. Shore the anatomy of improvisation, and so I wrote out a simple variant of a standard popular song and told her to learn to play the variant just as she would any other song. Later, I explained, she could make up her own variations; and finally, in the manner of true jazz musicians, she would be able to do this off the top of her head as she played.

The next week Mrs. Shore was so eager to show me what she had done that she could hardly wait for me to take off my topcoat. She had written words to the improvisation I had left with her to learn to play. I read her words a couple of times and sang them in my composer's voice. They worked quite well as a popular song lyric. I could see she had a knack for lyric writing, that hybrid art somewhere between light verse and serious poetry. She had never given songwriting a thought, she told me, and hadn't in the least intended to do this. The lyric had just sort of happened of its own accord. But I could see she was pleased I thought her words worked as a lyric.

But Mrs. Shore was my pupil, and I was supposed to be teaching her keyboard harmony and jazz piano. I wrote out another "improvisation" a little more involved than the first. I was pretty sure she would write another lyric, but to do so she would first have to learn how to play it, so I would be doing my duty as a music teacher.

The next week she presented me with three lyrics she had written to the second improvisation I had given her, and they were all good. Mrs. Shore was incredibly inventive and was obviously dammed up with lyrics to the bursting point. In accordance with my decision to keep Mrs. Shore working, I had this evening brought a couple of my original tunes and said to her that in view of her talent and enthusiasm we might as well spend a part of each lesson on writing. She was delighted. I urged her, however, not to get her hopes up too high about selling anything. "Why don't we just write for the fun of it and see what happens? There's nothing wrong with having songwriting as a hobby," I told her. But secretly I hoped for more.

Mrs. Shore listened to me politely, then set out to do things her own way. She bought stacks and stacks of sheet music and poured over them for hours, trying to determine what made the lyrics sell. Then she would write, and write, and write, always in a very "commercial" vein. None of this writing for the fun of it or songwriting as a hobby nonsense for her. "There's gold in them thar hills," she told me with a new glint in her eye.

She showed everything we wrote to everyone she knew. She would call her friends at eight o'clock in the morning before they got off to work and sing our latest hit to them. One day a man came to repair the drainpipe. Mrs. Shore was at the piano going over a new tune when suddenly a head appeared through the window and asked if that were something she had written. It turned out that the repairman was something of a songwriter himself. The two of them spent the rest of the morning comparing notes. No pun intended.

The reaction to our songs Mrs. Shore got from her friends was for the most part quite favorable. "If you ask me they're as good as anything you hear on the *Hit Parade*" was a fairly typical remark. And since everybody knows somebody, professional contacts were always being proffered. For example, "My cousin has a friend who used to do publicity work at Columbia

Records, and I imagine he could get Mitch Miller to look at some of your songs."

But Mrs. Shore was a perfectionist and felt she wasn't quite ready to tackle the publishers and record companies. The more she learned about lyric writing and the "pop market" the harder it was for her to meet her own standards. She would lie awake for hours sometimes trying to make a lyric come out right. She confided in me that ordinarily she was only a moderate drinker, perhaps having a glass or two of sherry, but that these days with disturbing frequency she had to tip toe downstairs at two or three in the morning and pour herself a couple of healthy slugs of Scotch in order to get off to sleep. And she confessed to me with some embarrassment that in church one Sunday while kneeling in congregational prayer she found her mind wandering off to some lyric she had been having an especially hard time with.

For my part, I had long since run out of old tunes to give her and was working like a beaver to have something new for her each week. If I lagged behind in this, she would present me with one or more lyrics that needed music. The team of Miles and Shore could work either way: music first, then lyrics, like Rodgers and Hart; or lyrics first, then music, like Rodgers and Hammerstein. And our original plan to spend only half of the lesson on songwriting and the other half on playing had gone by the board weeks earlier. The lessons were now pure Tin Pan Alley.

Even though the weather was now warm again, Mrs. Shore never talked about her flower garden any more. I noticed, in fact, that the garden, far from being the prettiest one in the neighborhood, was now actually going to seed. As for what was going on inside the house—the children had lost interest in staying up and listening to their mother play because, of course, she wasn't playing any more, only writing.

Even the big friendly collie had stopped being friendly and just sulked around. And Mr. Shore, arriving home from work, would march straight through the living room to the kitchen, hardly looking at me and stopping only long enough to give his wife a little pat. It seemed to me that now it was not so much a love pat as a solicitous one—a pat that said, "I know what you are going through, dear." And these nights after the lesson there was no ride back down to the subway station. I walked.

It was painfully evident that Mr. Shore saw me as the agent of his wife's decline. It was I who had turned her from a happy, well-functioning housewife into a half-crazed artist. I wondered if he was still in favor of women developing their talent. Certainly when he bought the piano he hadn't reckoned as part of the cost having his whole household turned upside down. Everything had been running smoothly until I came on the scene, therefore it was all my fault. I really think if I had been having an affair with Mrs. Shore and he had found out, he would have taken it with more equanimity.

One Monday night when I went out there at the appointed time, I knew right away that something was up. For one thing, Mr. Shore was home for a change. Mrs. Shore took me aside and told me they were going on a long cruise. She said she didn't really want to go because it would mean such a long hiatus in the lessons and the songwriting. She had argued with her husband at length about this, but he had insisted that they go.

I knew this was the end—of the music lessons and of the songwriting. The cruise was like those that wealthy fathers once sent their daughters on to get them away from and help them forget suitors considered unsuitable. I knew I was going to miss Mrs. Shore, her lyrics and her enthusiasm.

About a year later a friend introduced me to a young and eager composer who was looking for a lyric writer. He thought I might be able to help. I decided the best way I could do this would be to show him some of the songs I had written with different people and let him pick out the lyric writer he liked best. He read through several manuscripts without saying anything until he came to the songs with Mrs. Shore's lyrics. "This is the person I want to work with," he said emphatically. With the feeling that I was about to complicate several people's lives beyond hope of untangling, I gave him her phone number.

I saw this young composer again a few months later and asked how he and Mrs. Shore were getting along with their writing. "Fine," he said, "but it's funny. She wants to do everything by telephone or mail. I have yet to see the inside of her house." I could see that Mrs. Shore was now enjoying the best of both worlds—housewife and artist. I imagined her flower garden was once again the crown jewel of Jamaica Estates and that she, herself, once again looked elegant. As for Mr. Shore, I had no doubt he was getting along just fine.

10

Deadlines

*T*he hospitable family with whom I now found myself living rented out two rooms in addition to mine, giving me less privacy than I had enjoyed on Thomson Street after the climb up those stairs. Nor did I still have my piano. There was, however, a good solid upright in the jointly used living room. Surprisingly enough, between television shows and family gatherings of one kind or another, I managed to continue work on songs I had started while living on Thomson Street alone. But this catch-as-catch-can songwriting as a spare time activity was soon to change.

Back in Lexington, there had been a dancer named Gloria Stevens. I had not known her well but was aware that she had moved to New York some time before I had. I knew also that she had joined two other dancers and formed what was known as The Bob Hamilton Trio. This group had some success in the early days of television. One day, after all these years, I ran into Gloria on Eighth Avenue. Naturally we had a lot of catching up to do. In the process we got to know each other better than we ever had in Lexington. My songwriting was news to her, and I enjoyed playing some of my tunes in her apartment up on West End Avenue.

The timing was fortuitous. Two of Gloria's friends, John and Lynne Weiner, were owners of a summer resort in the famous Catskill Mountains of upstate New York. Here it was April, and the Weiners were still looking for a staff composer for the summer season, which began on the Fourth of July and ran through Labor Day. Gloria told them about having just become reacquainted with me and hearing some of my music. She said I impressed her as a real possibility for the person who could fill that position. The Weiners thanked her and said they would like to set up a meeting with their entertainment director, Richard Diamond, right away. The final decision would be his.

The meeting/audition with Mr. Diamond went quite well. After hearing a few of my songs, he said he thought my music would play quite well to Catskill audiences. On our next get-together a short time later he gave me a backlog of song lyrics needing music and also the libretto and song lyrics for a one-act musical theater work. All of this music would need to be completed by opening day, July Fourth, so that they could be learned and performed by the lead singers—two men and two women who were already engaged for the summer, along with a small instrumental ensemble, whose musical director was an experienced pianist named Freddie Johnson.

After settling in on July Fourth, Diamond and I would concentrate on completing a full-length two-act musical with at least eight songs. This show had to be finished and rehearsed so that it could be presented to the larger audiences that always filled the resort in August. With all of this writing in July, Diamond quipped that I might just have time for a very short dip in the lake every other day.

Wow! Even though, as I have said before, I am not very enterprising, I do like to rise to the occasion when called upon to do so. Obviously, the first thing to do now was come to some kind of agreement with my landlady that would give me more access to the living room piano. I knew without measuring that it would not fit into my small off-the-hall bedroom.

If I were given to extrasensory beliefs, I would say that at this point I was being looked after from afar. The person occupying the large room at the

Eighth Avenue end of the apartment was a singer. At about the time I am describing, the show she was in was closing in New York and preparing to go on the road. She was going with the show and so had to move out of this room. The timing was perfect. In the few days it took to get a piano mover, the singer was gone. The landlady lost no time in having the living room piano and me moved into the vacated room. That would be just about the last anybody saw of me until the end of June, at which time I headed for the Catskills.

The people I did see, of course, were Dick Diamond and Freddie Johnson. Working every evening and every weekend, I finished writing music for every song lyric Dick had given me, many of which were for a charming little one act show engagingly titled *Philomanda the Panda*. And Freddie Johnson was well into the arrangements for his small orchestral ensemble. It was at this time also that I met Freddie's charming wife, singer Louise Woods. Freddie and Louise had been actively involved in the first important black musical revue, *Shuffle Along*, written by Noble Sissle and Eubie Blake.

Working with Freddie and Louise I learned a lot about writing for the voice—such things as which melodic lines would work vocally and which would not. This has stood me in good stead ever since.

11

"Brother"

Located near the town of Livingston Manor, New York, was a "Catskill Resort" named White Roe. It had been established by John Weiner's parents on a large and lovely lake. "Ma" Weiner was still there, a dear matriarch rocking back and forth in front of her lakeside cottage. White Roe was where the comedian Danny Kaye had gotten his start. That was in the nineteen thirties, and Dick Diamond, as entertainment director, had been his supervisor.

I arrived at White Roe on July 1, 1955. John and Lynne Weiner and John's brother, Mac, made me feel at home right away, as did Dick Diamond. I was introduced to Tedd Browne, a good-looking Jamaican with a wonderful baritone voice. Tedd was one of the two male singers hired for the summer. He and I were directed to the room we were to share in a dormitory-like room near the lake.

By now it was time for dinner. I was told that, as staff composer, I would be eating every meal at the table near the front of the dining room with the Weiners and entertainment director, Dick Diamond. I was not used to such preferential treatment but soon managed to adapt myself to it. It reminded me of stories I had heard about people on a ship being seated at the captain's table during a cruise.

The next day Freddie Johnson and Louise Woods arrived, as did Rickie Carter, a California singer now living in New York. I was soon to meet the orchestral arranger and the other male singer, as well as Saul and Lenny, two Columbia University Law School students, who were taking the summer off to be Borscht Belt stand-up comedians.

July Fourth was here. Regular summer guests and newcomers rented their rooms and summer festivities were under way—swimming and boating in the lake, tennis and other games on the grounds. The theater was open. Rehearsals were scheduled during the day and performances given at night. The singers were doing their regular repertory plus some of the songs by Dick Diamond and me. The comics were doing their turns.

A favorite song of everyone's had a lyric by Lynne Weiner herself. She had given it to me the day I arrived, and I had set it to music immediately.

Blue Rendezvous
(© 1955)

Shadows and smoke and the mem'ry of you
Are all I have left of the rapture we knew.
Laughter was short, now I'm caught in a blue rendezvous.

When I'm alone it seems terribly wrong
To keep hearing music that once was our song.
There is no peace, no release from my blue rendezvous.

Some make light of love and joke of it,
But we were in love and never spoke of it.
My heart was gay, but when you went away
It broke of it, broke of it!

So much still lingers—the taste of your kiss.
How can I love again feeling like this?
And so I brood in the mood of my blue rendezvous.

Louise Woods sang this beautifully, both on stage and in the relaxed community room afterwards. There was also ballroom dancing there for those who enjoyed it.

Dick Diamond and I were busily putting the finishing touches on the musical fantasy, *Philomanda, the Panda*, which featured such songs as, "I'm Just a Little Melody A'waiting to be Born," "Captain Leander," and "I'm On My Own Veranda." I had read and heard that Catskills audiences were very hard to please. I was therefore especially glad to see that when we finished this hour of musical word play, it went over very well.

Then, of course, there were Dick's individual lyrics that I had been setting to music during April, May, and June. A few titles will suggest their flavor—"Conformity," "I'm Just Gonna Do a Tap Dance," "What's My Cue for Tonight?"

There was, however, one song by Dick Diamond that was in a class by itself. It was written for Jamaican baritone, Tedd Browne, and sung beautifully by him throughout the summer. As you read the words to this song, remember that they were written a few years before the Civil Rights Movement gathered full strength.

Brother
(used by permission)

Gonna sing me a song called "Brother"
It's a sin making skin be a badge I must wear
Of my sorrow.

Gonna sing me a song called "Brother"
It ain't true only you own the earth and what's left
I can borrow.

Now then, brother
Hear me, brother
They say Eve was everyone's mother.
Well, if Eve was everyone's mother,
Then, brother, ain't I your brother?

So as one free man to another—
Take my hand, understand
All I want is my share of tomorrow,
And I'll sing me a song called "Brother."

After leaving White Roe, Tedd Browne sang in restaurants and nightclubs in a number of cities. "Brother" was a staple of his repertory. I saw him once again in the mid 1960s when I was on a visit to my old hometown of Lexington. Not very long after that I was horrified and dismayed to learn that Tedd had gotten into a dispute with some MAFIA nightclub owners in Cleveland, and that they had settled the dispute by "taking him for a ride."

The summer at White Roe ended with the two-act musical finished, orchestrated, rehearsed, and performed. Like the song "Brother," it had a good deal of social consciousness written into it. The August audience seemed to love the show, and I felt we had finished the summer on a strong note.

On Labor Day, as I was leaving White Roe on my way to the bus stop, Ma Weiner, who had not said a word to me all summer, stopped rocking long enough to beckon me. I leaned over and she said, "You done good." I felt this was an accolade, a perfect end to a memorable summer.

12

Chandler Warren and the Columbia Law Revues

When, on July 2,1955, I had left the city to fill my position as staff composer at White Roe, I had had to give up my room in the apartment on Eighth Avenue and West 56th Street. Returning on Labor Day I just "fell into" the first place I could find in the neighborhood, which was a cheap, rundown rooming house on West 56th Street near Ninth Avenue.

I was now without a piano, but fortune continued to smile on me, as the saying goes. I was, of course, keeping in touch with Freddie Johnson and Louise Woods by visiting them in their apartment during the week and going to hear them perform on weekends in a small nightclub called the Crazy Bear. This was an unpretentious one-room club on the ground floor of a building on Sixth Avenue in the Forties. Louise was still singing my songs, and Freddie's backing of them on piano had become more and more complex and interesting.

Being the first-rate musician that he was, Freddie owned a large grand piano that was too big to fit into his and Louise's apartment. He therefore rented a long, narrow room in the old Columbia Broadcasting System building on Broadway at Fiftieth Street. Freddie gave me a key to the room and said I could use the piano on evenings and weekends. Since he used it mostly on weekdays when I was at work, this was a good arrangement. His generosity would have been most welcome at any time, but it was especially important now in view of what happened next.

Saul and Lenny, the two stand-up comedian law school students at White Roe, had been telling me all summer about a law school student friend of theirs named Chandler Warren, who, in their opinion, was a very good poet and playwright. They had also told Chandler about me, and it was at just about the time I was given the use of Freddie's piano that this meeting took place.

Chandler is a genial, easygoing fellow with an engaging sense of humor. I felt compatible with him right away. When I read some of his work, I saw immediately what Saul and Lenny had been talking about. Chan and I started meeting at Freddie's piano whenever we could and would work for two or three hours. He would lean against the side of that long grand piano and listen to me play some of my tunes. My playing was still "modest," to use a polite word. When I played a melody he liked especially, Chan would pull out a pad and start writing. He would then ask that I play a certain musical phrase again, and then again.

It was in this way that the first song we wrote together came into being. It was a tune I had been carrying around in my head and on music manuscript paper for quite some time. Fittingly enough, this first song of ours was called "Words."

Words
(© 1955)

Words try to tell the old story.
Words try to sing of love's glory.
Loving words, tender words
Try it ev-'ry day, but
Being words, only words
How much can they say?

Words try to help my lips teach you.
Words try to help my arms reach you; but
The more I say the less I say—
What am I to do? for
Words just can't tell how I love you.

Over the years Chandler and I have written many individual songs in this way; that is, he has "found" the right words inherent in many of my melodies. But here, nearing the end of 1955 and heading into 1956, he was intent on writing a musical theater work—a Columbia Law Revue, not to be confused with the periodical publication "The Law Review." In this determination Chan was aided and abetted by fellow law students, Saul and Lenny, whose writing credits would be Saul Turtletaub and Leonard Korobkin. Those two talented gentlemen would help write some of the dialog between songs and would also choreograph the movements of the participating faculty and students. In the nature of the case the words of the songs, with their legal terminology and inside-school references, would be written first.

Soon after the first of the year in 1956, I was able to extricate myself from the rundown rooming house on West 56th Street and move into a third floor walk-up apartment on the south side of West 48th Street between Seventh and Eighth Avenues. This apartment had a large living room and two small bedrooms. There was a baby grand piano in the middle of the living room. Its owner was the other tenant, who had a night job.

This was a good arrangement for me. Chandler and I now had no further need for Freddie's piano; we could use the baby grand in the living room. We got to work right away, going over the music I was setting to the lyrics he was writing for the Law Revue, songs with such titles as, "We Lawyers Are So Legal" and "You, Baby, You're No Bargain And Sale." We worked on evenings and weekends until we felt the show was ready. Rehearsals could now begin.

A former Columbia Law School graduate, Lanny Ross, was now, in

1956, a successful popular singer. He was to be the star attraction in this first ever Law Revue. Freddie Johnson was the musical director of an ensemble made up of piano, bass, drums, a trumpet, and two tenor saxophones. Another holdover from White Roe taking part in the show was the wonderful singer, Rickie Carter. Saul and Lenny would be on stage, as would other students and faculty, poking fun at themselves and at each other.

All of this came together in the late spring of 1956 on the stage of a small auditorium on the Columbia University campus. The rousing opening number said it all—

Hi there! The law revue's singing to you!
We're the first law revue. How do you do?

Hey there! A raw revue we're bringing too;
And it's fun wringing some money from you.

Clients who come to us will all say
Our briefs look just like the script for a play.

Actors we may not be, but we can try.
So, please, bear with us folks;
Laugh at our corny jokes.
And so, let's go; on with the show!

There were several fully attended performances, and the reception was enthusiastic. Norman Nadel, critic on the New York *World Telegram and Sun*, called Miles and Warren the new Rodgers and Hart and gave the show a wonderful review. This, of course, thrilled us no end. And the Columbia College newspaper, *The Spectator*, raved about the show as well.

In 1957 Chandler and I wrote a second Columbia Law School Revue. This one was called, *The Blackstone Jungle*. Many of the people from the first Law Revue participated. In addition, this year's show featured June Warren, wife of Dean William S. Warren. Chandler and I wrote two songs just for her: "Oh, How I'd Like to Get to Know You" and "Put Down that Briefcase, Baby."

June had been a chorus girl in London's West End musical theater during World War II. It was then and there that William S. Warren met her and they fell in love and were married. Her maiden name was June Peel, and she was a cousin by marriage to Lady Peel, better known as Beatrice Lillie.

The opening number of the second revue was the same as that of the first, except that the second line became, "We're the new Law Revue; How Do You Do?" In addition to the songs written for June Warren, this second revue featured such songs as, "On the Corner of Broad and Wall" with an underlying calypso rhythm and "The Kent Hall Rock" with a kind of rock underpinning.

This second show was performed in the MacMillan Theater on the campus, a much larger venue than the one used in 1956. Many university students and faculty saw it, and the reception was as enthusiastic, if not more so, than it had been the year before.

A musical Law Revue has been written and produced at Columbia University every spring since those long-ago years, 1956-57. They have long been a fixture at the school. The two revues described here were the first such shows at any law school in the country. The word of their success and the success of such shows in subsequent years got around. The result is that today these revues are an annual kind of celebration at many law schools in the U.S.

13

Tin Pan Alley and Songs as Products

etween 1950, when my G.I. Bill of Rights expired and I had to leave the Julliard School of Music, and 1955, when I started writing musical theater works at the Catskills summer resort, I spent most of my spare time trying to have my songs accepted by a music publisher. I was told by those in the know that in order to do this I would have to "freeze my tail off in front of the Brill Building," that bastion of music publishers located on Broadway and 49th Street in New York, right in the heart of "Tin Pan Alley."

"Would doing that make my songs better?" I asked myself. There were certainly enough other hopefuls standing out there in the cold. One day I asked one of these denizens if he had seen a certain person I was looking for. "Bert didn't come in today" was his answer.

It was becoming pretty obvious that if I wanted to have my songs accepted by a publisher I would have to start thinking of them as products to be bought and sold. But wait a minute. When, as a young teenager I had sat on the front porch on a summer evening and listened to *Hit Parade* songs from the radio across the street, was I listening to products? Does the guy who, in the twilight, sings his favorite love song to his sweetheart think of that song as a product?

To be sure, the contemporary record is more than just a song. It is a complex amalgam of song, arrangement, electronic instruments, and engineering. As such, it could be regarded as a product, and often a very interesting and appealing one. Still, to me, the mindset that thinks of music as a product is uncongenial.

On one of my first forays into the Brill Building, I found myself in an elevator car with the great songwriter and singer, Johnny Mercer. This reminded me of the time not too long before that I had ridden in an elevator with Eleanor Roosevelt in the building on West 57th Street that housed Radio Free Europe. On that occasion, I managed to utter a few words of admiration before leaving the elevator. But in the Brill Building elevator with Johnny Mercer I found myself completely tongue-tied.

That day in the Brill Building might have been the time I was on my way to see the publisher who said, "You've got to write songs that start at the top of the octave because that's where the song on Eddie Fischer's latest hit record started." This advice and other pronouncements similar to it persuaded me that music publishers were too often chasing their own tails. This commercial mindset—that you should always follow the latest trend—militates against the creative person's writing what he or she honestly feels when he or she honestly feels it, a prerogative I had no intention of giving up.

Closely related to the commercial habit of mind is the competitive disposition, which at times can manifest itself in very disagreeable behavior. One day near my apartment, I was about to pass a songwriting team, composer and lyricist, who I knew only by sight. They stopped me because one of them had momentarily mistaken me for the big band orchestral arranger, Eddie Sauter. Seeing his mistake, he apologized. I told him it was no problem, that I had been mistaken for Sauter before.

His partner stuck his face close to mine and asked in a challenging tone, "Can you *write* like Eddie Sauter?" I wanted to say that it wasn't I who said I looked like him, but just said, "I admire him very much, but I'm a songwriter, not an arranger."

"Can you *write* like Eddie Sauter?" he yelled back over his shoulder as they moved on.

14

Wedo's Music Copying Service

Located on the south side of West Forty-Ninth Street between Broadway and Eighth Avenue was Wedo's Music Copying Service—founded, owned and operated by Wedo Marasco, a saxophone-playing alumnus of the Vaughn Monroe Orchestra. I could still freeze my tail off in front of the Brill Building, cross West Forty-Ninth Street and climb a flight of stairs to the warmth, in every sense, of Wedo's.

Being in Tin Pan Alley, one part of Wedo's business was having his staff of musicians copy out instrumental parts for saxophones, clarinets and other instruments of the orchestra that arrangers had made to be recorded by the leading vocalists of the day—Perry Como, Doris Day etc. The other major part of his business was having his staff copy instrumental parts from orchestral arrangements that had been made for New York theater pit orchestras. After all this important work, Wedo's still had time for songwriters like me, who came in off the street and wanted machine-made copies of their songs to show to those music publishers in the Brill Building across the street and elsewhere.

I have many fond memories of Wedo's, beginning in 1948, the year I moved to New York and enrolled at the Julliard School of Music. During my last two years in Lexington, the piano teacher I finally found was a talented and understanding woman named Elizabeth Logan Tyler. Her son, Jim, was a very talented composer and orchestral arranger. He was very supportive and encouraging to me in my beginning attempts to become a songwriter. Jim moved to New York a few months before I did and began supporting himself as a copyist of recording and orchestral scores at Wedo's. It was only natural, then, that, when I moved to New York a few months later and sought Jim out, I was given an insider's introduction to Wedo. Jim, however, wouldn't work there much longer as a copyist because he was beginning to have some success as an orchestral arranger for Broadway musicals.

I, however, continued to be a frequent customer for a few years and then, at Wedo's repeated requests, and because I welcomed the opportunity, I gave up my position at Radio Free Europe and began working for him. I was not a copiest. Instead, I operated the reproducing machines and delivered the copied scores to record companies for their recording sessions and to Broadway theaters for their upcoming productions. This gave me a speaking acquaintance with the important songwriters and orchestral arrangers of the day—Burt Bachrach, Stanley Applebaum, and Dave Grusin, to name only three.

However, most important to me was the support and encouragement I got from the other employees, some habitués of the company, and from Wedo himself. Many of these—Jerry Bass, Arnold Wertheimer, Vic Harrington, Russ Goudey, Carl Beyer, and Bob Holloway—were accomplished instrumentalists and/or arrangers themselves. I benefited greatly from the willingness of all these colleagues to listen to the songs I was writing and to offer their constructive criticism.

Being the creative and imaginative people they were, Wedo and a few of his co-workers formed a music publishing company and gave it the name Consonant Music, Inc. At about the same time, copyist and excellent orchestral arranger Bob Holloway introduced me to an impressively good West Coast singer named Bob Davis. Bob Holloway in his spare time was helping Bob Davis form an orchestra that would back up his singing on a recording they planned to make.

Imagine my delight when Wedo and the other Consonant Music officials selected a song of mine they wanted to publish, have arranged by Bob Holloway, and recorded by what would now be called the Bob Davis Orchestra. The song they picked was one I had written a few years earlier with Shirley Shore, the Queens housewife who had transformed my weekly keyboard harmony lessons with her into busy songwriting sessions.

The Bob Holloway arrangement of the song was appropriate and beautiful, as was the vocal by Bob Davis. Delighted as I would have been in any case, it was especially beneficial to me that the publication and recording of this song qualified me to become a member of ASCAP, the American Society of Composers, Authors, and Publishers, and of NARAS, the National Academy of Recording Arts and Sciences.

A happy reminder of those long-ago days came to me in February 2008 in the form of a certificate stating:

The New York Chapter of the National Academy of Recording Arts and Sciences is honored to bestow Robert Miles a lifetime membership in the recording academy in recognition of more than thirty-five years of continuous service to and support of the academy and its education, advocacy and human service initiatives.

My Life Begins With You
(© 1952, © renewed 1980)

This is the end of sad romances,
This is the end of week-end dances,
This is the end of backward glances.
My life begins with you.

This is the love I needed badly,
This is the love I yearned for madly,
This is the love I welcome gladly.
My life begins with you.

I can see that this was meant to be,
You and you alone for me.
You were heaven-sent to me,
The angels' answer to my lonely plea.

This is the start of sunny weather
And many happy years together.
This is the start of our forever.
My life begins with you.

15

Jeanne

I met Jeanne the way people met in old Hollywood movies. I was invited to a New Year's Eve party being given by an old friend who lived in a small apartment near Washington Square. Not being very gregarious, I had greeted a few people I knew and then gone to a small adjacent room and seated myself at the baby grand piano there. After leafing through the sheet music on top of the instrument, I began to quietly play a few of my own songs, more for my own satisfaction than with any idea of attracting attention to myself.

After I had been playing for ten minutes or so, a slender, good looking, and soft-spoken woman came over and asked me what it was I was playing. I told her they were my songs, co-written with several different lyric writers. She seemed genuinely interested and, after listening to a few more, had some very complimentary things to say about several of them. By now it was time to ring in the New Year, and she and I rejoined the rest of the party. Not long after that the celebration came to an end, but not before Jeanne gave me her phone number, which I intended to use very soon thereafter.

However, I didn't feel completely free to call her for several months. I thought about her constantly, but I was using this time to divest myself of other attachments and obligations. Then, just as I felt ready to call Jeanne, my sister Marian, who was living with her husband in Albuquerque, New Mexico, called and asked me to bring our mother from her home in Lexington out to Albuquerque for what could be one last visit. The reason for this request was that our mother was beginning to show signs of dementia.

Appreciating the importance of this request, I went to Kentucky and accompanied Mother on a flight from there to Albuquerque. I visited with my sister and her husband for a few days, assessing our mother's condition; then, being that far west, indulged myself in a flight to Los Angeles, a city I had always wanted to visit. While there I looked up my old friend, Nancy Van Norman, whom I had known when at the Julliard School of Music. Her married name is Nancy Bloomer Deussen. She is an accomplished and successful composer of serious vocal and instrumental music. Nancy and I had a very satisfying visit after which I returned to Albuquerque and escorted my mother back to her Kentucky home. Getting myself back to New York, I finally called Jeanne.

She and I had not learned very much about each other in our brief encounter on New Year's Eve. Now, as we started going out together, I learned that after divorcing her husband in Santa Fe, New Mexico, she had moved to New York with her two children, Kenneth twelve and Dana eleven. They had settled into a comfortable seventh-floor apartment on West 85th Street between Broadway and West End Avenue. One nice thing about this location was that Kenneth and Dana could play after school and on weekends in nearby Riverside Park.

Jeanne had an advertising job with an advertising firm on Madison Avenue. She was also active in Democratic politics. I was working at Wedo's Music Copying Service and, of course, writing music at night and on weekends. Even with all this, Jeanne and I enjoyed a few quiet get-togethers every week. We enjoyed getting to know each other, and I enjoyed getting to know Kenneth and Dana and their getting to know me. Now and then,

Jeanne and I would venture out to hear music, either a concert at Lincoln Center or a cabaret singer like Steve Ross, Ronny Whyte, Blossom Dearie, or Jane Scheckter, all favorites of mine. These outings were especially gratifying when Steve, Ronny, Blossom or Jane included a song of mine in their program.

This leisurely courtship, to use a conventional term, went on for almost two years. On May 5, 1962, feeling that it was both right and gratifyingly welcome to both of us at this point in our lives, we were married in a small Presbyterian church on upper Park Avenue by a minister, who years before had been a friend of my father's, also a Presbyterian minister. A solo from Haydn's oratorio, "The Creation," was sung by Jeanne's next-door apartment neighbor, Otto Hammer. Otto was a member of the Metropolitan Opera Chorus. The wedding reception in Jeanne's—now Jeanne's and my—apartment was festive and happy. A few of my old friends and a number of new ones I had met through Jeanne were in attendance. I felt that this marriage was getting off to a happy and auspicious start.

16

Moving In

I had for several weeks been moving things from my apartment on East 65th Street into my new West 85th Street lodging. Now, being married, it was time to move myself and the rest of my belongings, most especially my upright piano.

I had acquired this instrument while still living on West 48th Street. At about the time Chandler Warren and I finished writing the first Law Revue, the owner of the small concert grand on which we wrote it moved out of the apartment, taking that instrument with him. Soon after that, I was able to acquire a small upright piano that served me well the rest of the time I lived at that address.

Between then and the time I married Jeanne, I lived in three different apartments into each of which the piano had to be hoisted: East 14th Street between First and Second Avenues, top floor; corner of East 93rd Street and Second Avenue, top floor; and corner of East 65th Street and Second Avenue, ground floor.

My new home on West 85th Street was the right size to accommodate one additional person. But a piano? The apartment opened onto a narrow hall that led to a reasonably large living room. Immediately on the right of this hall was one entrance to the kitchen. Another hall led from the living room to the rear of the apartment. The first door on the left opened into the master bedroom. On the right was another entrance to the kitchen. The next door on the right was the bathroom. At the end of the hall on the left was Kenneth's bedroom; on the right was Dana's.

Our first plan had been to wrestle the piano to the left side of the entrance hall, across from the first entrance to the kitchen. It is true that this hall would have accommodated the instrument, but placing it there would have meant that immediately upon entering the front door people would have had to walk sideways to get by it.

What about the living room then? The sofa and easy chairs were comfortably arranged there. The only possible place for the piano would have been a corner that was used as a dining area when the big, round kitchen table was not being used for that purpose.

O.K. that left Jeanne's and my bedroom. I was reminded of the time fifteen years earlier in my old hometown of Lexington, right after I had married my first wife Pat. We had been offered the use of an apartment replete with an upright piano in the bedroom. This had turned me off right away, and I had moved the piano into the kitchen, wanting to leave the living room free for quiet, academic study. But here at 252 West 85th Street, New York City, there was no possibility of, nor desire to move the piano into the kitchen. So into the bedroom it went. Having it there did not turn me off as it had back in Lexington. If anything, it turned me on, for I wrote a number of individual songs on it there and one musical theater work.

The truth is that one of the first songs I wrote there on the bedroom piano is one of my all-time favorite Warren and Miles songs. It is a ballad for which Chandler Warren wrote the following beautiful and expressive words:

Tell Me Softly
(© 1983 by Warchan Music Co., ASCAP)

Tell me softly,
Tell me gently,
Let me know that you care.

Say it sweetly,
Say it clearly,
Say you always will be there.

If you say it from your heart,
What could ever keep us apart?

I will tell you very softly
With a heart that is true
I will always, simply always love you.

Tell me softly,
Tell me slowly.
If you whisper, I'll hear.

Say it truly
That you love me
And you always will be near.

There's no reason we should hide
What we're feeling deep down inside.

I will tell you very softly with a heart that is true
I will always, simply always love you.

17

Kentucky Sojourns

My happy and musically productive first two years of marriage was interrupted by a turn for the worse in my mother's mental condition, which first manifested itself in 1960 when I had flown her from her home in Lexington out to New Mexico for a short visit with my sister, whose husband was stationed there at the time.

Now, in the spring of 1964 she had gone to visit her sister and two brothers in Roanoke, Virginia. Attempting to return home, she had gotten herself stranded in Lexington, Virginia, having no idea where she was. She had mistaken Lexington, Virginia for Lexington, Kentucky.

I felt a strong need to go to Lexington and see for myself what could be done. I wanted to be sure that she had the best professional help available. I also wanted to see if my presence would help her. This was to be the first of two sojourns to Lexington—one in 1964, the other in 1965, each lasting a few months. I have always, and will always be grateful to and in admiration of Jeanne for putting up with these long absences with as much equanimity as she did. Neither of us, certainly, were prepared for these lengthy interruptions so early in our married life.

These protracted visits with my mother in Lexington were a mixture of satisfaction in feeling that I was helping her and depression caused by being away from New York, Jeanne, Kenneth, and Dana. On my first visit I spent time reminiscing, helping Mother remember important and happy times in our past. She was still able to enjoy listening to music, so I took her to evening recitals or concerts from time to time given by visiting artists. She had forgotten that I had become a songwriter, so I didn't burden her with stories about that.

On this first visit I had a part-time day job—cataloguing special collections, many of them pertaining to music, for the University of Kentucky Library. This, in a small way, was my first attempt to use my academic education, however tangentially, in my work.

After a few months, yearning to get back home and feeling that my mother would be all right without me for a while, especially if my brother, who lived in Cincinnati, Ohio, eighty miles away, would check on her periodically, I returned to New York and family. I began right away to look for a meaningful job, but as nothing turned up right away, I settled for an afternoon and evening job as a sales clerk in the elegant Doubleday Book Store, located on Fifth Avenue near 57th Street.

If one must have a menial job, this one was pleasant enough. I enjoyed working among books, brushing up on the classics and reading enough about the new ones to answer questions intelligently. I also enjoyed seeing old friends and acquaintances who would come in once in a while to browse, having no idea, of course, that I was there. From time to time also, there would be a celebrity shopper. I was so pleased one night to be able to find the book that the great American composer Aaron Copeland had asked for.

What prompted my second sojourn to Lexington was some pressure I was beginning to feel from my aunt and uncles (Mother's sister and brothers) in Roanoke, Virginia. They had decided it was time to move their older sister to a nursing home in Roanoke. I, rightly or wrongly, wanted to decide for myself when that should be. The only way I could make that determination was to go back down to Lexington and stay with her. Once again, Jeanne was very tolerant of what could be regarded as an unreasonable decision on my part.

On this second sojourn in 1965, I stayed with Mother during the day and worked late into the night as a proofreader on the morning newspaper, the *Lexington Herald*. That job could be said to be another step in the direction of using my education in my employment.

More to the point in that regard was my writing for the paper an occasional review of programs given in Lexington by visiting performers. One I remember was the popular pianist of that time, Erroll Garner. Another was the famous Hollywood composer, Henry Mancini. He told Hollywood stories and played his music on a grand piano in a large auditorium at the University of Kentucky before a capacity audience. What I now remember most about the evening was that, when he finished playing his last number, Mancini got up from the piano stool, took a few steps to the left and started vigorously kicking one of the front legs of the piano. He then walked around and kicked the other front leg before bowing to the audience and walking off the stage. I, of course, included this in my review.

All during this second sojourn, which lasted several months into 1966, I had many periods of feeling depressed. First, there was my mother's mental condition, which was deteriorating before my very eyes. Then, of course, the longer I was away from New York the more I missed Jeanne, Ken, and Dana. Finally in the spring of 1966, I was ready to agree that it was time for Mother to give up her apartment and be moved to a nursing home in Roanoke, where she would be near her two brothers and sister. A younger sister, who lived in Wisconsin, came to Lexington and helped me pack all of Mother's belongings and close down the apartment. After a sad farewell, this sister took Mother to Virginia, and I returned to my home in New York.

On this last sojourn to Lexington, the only access I had to a piano was an occasional visit to a practice room in the music department at the University of Kentucky. There, from time to time, I managed to write a few songs, most notably this one, for which I wrote both words and music. It was, of course, written for Jeanne.

All of My Life
(© 1965, © renewed 1993)

All of my life
I have known that my life was all wrong,
But I couldn't change it.

All of my life
I've been singing a blue kind of song,
Couldn't rearrange it.

All that I saw was out of focus
'Til you filled the frame.
Love worked its magic hokus pokus,
Now nothing is the same.

All of my life
I'll be trying to make up for the days
I didn't know about you.

All of my life
I'll be happily learning the ways
I can't live without you.

All of those empty years I had to
Are now beyond recall.
You are my life, you're my love, my all.

All of those years I ate my heart out
Are now beyond recall.
You are my life, you're my love, my all.

18

Gainful Employment

It was, of course, great to get back home in mid-1966. Although I felt sad about my mother's condition, I also felt that I had done as much for her as I was able to and that she would now be well looked after in a facility designed to care for people in her condition. I was also glad that she was back in her original hometown where her brothers and sister could look in on her frequently.

I had "inherited" my mother's aging Pontiac automobile, which now came in handy, because soon after getting home I applied for and got a position teaching English to adult students at Hofstra University on Long Island. The classes met at night and the Pontiac got me back and forth. In this position I did, of course, make use of my education. I enjoyed working with these adults who wanted to supplement their previous education by going back to school at night. I especially enjoyed reading and evaluating the papers I had assigned them to write.

My employment at Hofstra was, however, for one semester only. But this fact coincided nicely with the need I felt for a more permanent teaching position and one nearer to home. What looked as though it might be an opportunity of this kind came in the form of the Intensive Teacher Training Program sponsored by the New York City Board of Education in their effort to recruit new teachers. The program was conducted in the summer of 1967 on a campus that later became the Queensboro Community College, a branch of City University of New York.

I was now forty-seven years old. Most of my fellow trainees were, as might be expected, in their twenties. During breaks between learning sessions, they would throw Frisbees back and forth and listen to The Beatles. I remember one applicant urging me to listen to them.

In this training program, I learned a lot about secondary school curricula and lesson plans. There was also much emphasis on discipline. The teacher must learn to enter the classroom with an air of authority. Body language was very important. At the end of the summer, one of the instructors took me aside and said, "Miles, with your temperament you will never make it in the classroom." As things turned out, I should have listened to him, but at this point I was all geared up to give it a try.

That fall I was assigned to the Frederick Douglass Intermediate School in Harlem. The school was named after the great nineteenth century abolitionist. I was given a sixth grade English class and a daily curriculum to follow. What success I did have was offset by my having to dodge wads of rolled-up who-knows-what whenever I turned to write something on the blackboard. And the noise in the classroom never fully abated. As a result, the teacher in the classroom adjacent to mine complained to the school principal and I was assigned to a class in another part of the building.

When, after a short time, it became abundantly clear that I could not maintain discipline in the classroom, I was assigned as an assistant to the school librarian. The head librarian, Miss Wilson, was a kind and capable person.

Also, as I remember, the students in the library, who wanted quiet so that they could read, helped to dissuade their fellow students from being noisy.

However, when Miss Wilson had to be away for any length of time, all hell broke loose. If two students got into an argument, books might be used as weapons and hurled back and forth. The library had recently added an audiovisual component to its collection. It being 1970, this consisted of reel-to-reel tapes of spoken-word books and the tape machines on which to play them. The library was located on the ground floor in the rear of one of the classroom buildings. There was a row of windows looking out on to a broad walkway about eight feet below. One day several students decided to amuse themselves by throwing several of these tape machines out of the windows on to this walk. This, of course, damaged the machines beyond repair.

Not long after this, some students decided it would be fun to lock me in the library director's office. I don't remember now how long I was trapped there or how I got out. I do remember that it was at about this time I resolved to work toward a degree in library science. With such a degree I would be able to apply for a position as an academic librarian on the college level. Despite all the misadventures I had suffered in the Frederick Douglass school library, I had found that library work was congenial to me. So it was that soon thereafter I started taking evening classes in library science at Rutgers University in nearby New Brunswick, New Jersey. At the beginning of the next academic year I transferred to evening classes at the Columbia University School of Library Science, from which, in 1972, I was granted the coveted Masters of Library Science Degree.

Looking back over the years at the Harlem secondary school experience I have just described, I can honestly say that, as difficult as it was and as battered as it left me, I had at the time it was happening in some way never felt so alive. I was living and working with vital, vibrant, radiant people, who had many odds against them. And despite all the problems, there were a few students every semester who told me how glad they were I was there and how much they had learned. I have never regretted the experience.

19

From Upright to Baby Grand

Upon receiving the degree in Library Science, I applied for, and was granted the position of Acquisitions Librarian at Medgar Evers College. This unit of the City University of New York was named after the famous civil rights leader and was located in the Crown Heights section of Brooklyn, not far from the Brooklyn Public Library and Prospect Park.

At roughly the same time, Jeanne was given a position with the Human Resources Administration of the City of New York. This entailed working in other boroughs than Manhattan, one of them being Brooklyn. Accordingly, we looked for, and found, a third floor walk-up apartment in the Boerum Hill section of Brooklyn, near downtown Brooklyn. Jeanne and I, Kenneth and Dana said "goodbye" to upper Manhattan and hired a moving van.

The last piece of furniture to be moved was my old Mathushek upright piano. This instrument, which had already had more than its share of moving adventures, now got stuck in the stairwell halfway between the first and second floors of our newly acquired walk-up apartment in Brooklyn.

There was nothing for the movers to do now but wrestle it back down the stairs to the ground floor and put it out of the way under the stairs.

The piano was now resting just outside the apartment of an accomplished pianist, who happened to be without an instrument at this time. So although I was to spend the next few months without a piano, my family and I could now listen to the strains of such compositions as the Brahms B-Flat Piano Concerto wend their way up the stairs and into our apartment. All the family had ever heard before from that little piano were my simple melodies.

I could now use the unmanueverability of the upright piano as a valid reason for acquiring a grand piano, which turned on its side would be able to make it up the stairs. But how was I to find a small grand piano that I could afford? After months of looking without any luck, one of our old friends from West 85th Street, Jeanne Eisenberg, put me together with an old friend of hers, a woman who had been the head of the music division of the Philadelphia Public Library, but who was now retiring and moving to Florida and into an apartment too small to accommodate even her five-foot baby grand piano.

She had owned this instrument since it was new, a Philadelphia made Lester piano, a company long out of business; and she had spent many happy hours, many happy years playing chamber music on it with her Philadelphia friends. Having to give the piano up now was causing her no little sadness. It was not surprising, therefore, that she wanted to meet the person who wanted to buy it. Not even Jeanne Eisenberg's endorsement was good enough . . . I had to pass the test myself.

So my Jeanne and I went to Philadelphia and spent a very pleasant hour or so with Mrs. Elizabeth Hartman in one of the old, genteel parts of the city. The piano was just what I wanted in both sound and appearance. I loved its delicate legato. Jeanne and I seemed to pass muster, and the piano changed hands for the very reasonable price of five hundred dollars. With the piano came the commodious music bench with its embroidered seat cushion. There was a special fluorescent light that also served as a music rack. I was even given the original brochure and guarantee, now thirty-six-years old. I was buying this 1933 made instrument in 1969.

Arranging to have the piano moved was costly in several ways. I had to spend a small fortune in phone calls to coordinate the operations of two different unions—one that would move the instrument from Philadelphia to the sidewalk in front of our apartment in Brooklyn—the other that would carry it from there up into our recently acquired top floor apartment. Without this delicate act of coordination, the piano would have been left on the sidewalk at the foot of the concrete stairs leading up to the entrance of 434 Pacific Street. But it all worked out. Now, with this vintage baby grand piano safely installed, I could get back to writing music.

20

Four O'clock Children

Not long after getting settled in the Brooklyn apartment, I saw in a trade paper a notice for an upcoming workshop, Writing for the Musical Theater, to be conducted at the Herbert Bergoff (HB) Studios on the Lower East Side of Manhattan.

The workshop was to be conducted by George Taros, a very accomplished pianist and all-'round musician. Many years later, I found George playing piano in a hotel lounge in Santa Fe, New Mexico. At this later date he was using his full name, George Koumantaros. In Santa Fe all those years later George was once again a great help to me in critiquing and making demonstration recordings of some of my musical theater works.

I will say here, parenthetically, that during the years I am describing I was (and am) still writing with Chandler Warren, but most of it was (and is) long distance. Chandler had established himself as a lawyer in the entertainment business. He was, and is, practicing this profession in his own firm in Los Angeles. A full account of our work together is given elsewhere in this autobiography.

Back in 1970 in the HB Studios, I found myself pairing off with Roberta

Kassan, known by friends as "Bobbie." She was a guidance counselor in the New York City Public School System. I could certainly have used her help there, but now I was grateful for the good and imaginative libretti and lyrics she was giving me to work with here. With this material and with George Koumantaros' criticism and guidance, I felt that I might be getting better at writing theatrical music. The accompanying musical figures were fuller, as was the incidental music under some of the dialog.

The HB Studios also supplied the performers for the next show I was to write. In 1967 I had been introduced to a poet and librettist named Arnold Falleder, who had just completed a one-hour original and poetic play entitled *Four O'Clock Children* (© 1968 and 1970, © renewed 1996). The cast was two boys, two girls, and a woman who doubled as the mother and another woman. The narrator's opening statement and the words to the first song give a sense of the unique charm of this show:

Narrator: This is a story called "Four O'Clock Children." It is about different kinds of children—children who may be very much like you, and others too. It all begins one afternoon in the playground of a park in the middle of a city. It could be your city or a different one; that is not important. Boy and Girl live in this park. They have always lived here and always will. As the play opens they enter from the wings hopping and singing a song.

My eyes see near, my eyes see far,
The moon's a monkey on blue bars.
The moon's a monkey on blue bars.
My eyes see near, my eyes see far.

My eyes see near, my eyes see far,
The cloud's milk-bone, the sky is tar.
The cloud's milk-bone, the sky is tar.
My eyes see near, my eyes see far.

In this one-act, fifty-minute show, the music is almost continuous. There is some spoken dialog, but it is short, poetic, and rhythmic, and the music under it leads easily into song, in many of which the lines are sung successively by each of the four young characters. Many of these songs are reprised and sung by all four children together. There is one song near the end of the show that is written in three-part counterpoint with one girl singing one line, the second girl singing the second line, and the two boys singing the third line. Writing the music for this show helped extend my ability to write for the musical theater.

The first production of *Four O'Clock Children* was in June 1969 by the Riverside Theater Workshop of Saint John's Episcopal Church. The director was Luigia Miller. Staging and choreography—very important in this show—were by Sally Bowden. Several members of the cast assembled for this first production came from George Koumantaros' HB Studios workshops: Jane Scheckter took the part of Annie, Gene Barrett was The Boy, and Martin Kenny was Jack. Carroll Godsman played The Girl. The parts of The Lady and The Mother were taken by Franca Sparacio. The show was enthusiastically received and was repeated many times at the church.

Four O'Clock Children was next produced in April 1970 at the Henry Street Settlement Playhouse on the Lower East Side of Manhattan. This production came about because an old friend of Jeanne 's from Santa Fe was now in New York, supporting herself and two daughters by playing piano professionally. This friend, Ruth Young, also did volunteer work at the Henry Street Settlement. It was her idea to mount the show there, and she was the musical director and pianist for that production. Her daughter, Beth, took the part of The Girl.

Our friend, Jeanne Eisenberg, who had enabled me to buy the baby grand piano from her Philadelphia friend, took the parts of The Lady and The Mother. As Jeanne Schlegel, she acted and sang in regional theater productions. Her husband, Herb Eisenberg, played trumpet in pit orchestras for Broadway musicals. Jeanne loved *Four O'Clock Children* and was just right as The Lady and The Mother.

I was soon to learn that this show worked just as well "in the round" as on stage. One day the first producer of the show, Luigia Miller, ran into a fellow tenant in the elevator—Menachem Dworman, proprietor of the Olive Tree Café, a coffeehouse on MacDougal Street in the Greenwich Village section of Manhattan. When she described the show to him, he said he thought it might work in the round at the Olive Tree on Saturday and Sunday afternoons.

In anticipation of this happening, Arnold Falleder and I wrote a new song for The Lady to sing.

> *I am old enough now to know*
> *I'd like to know*
> *Children like you*
>
> *And I'm young enough now to see*
> *Children like you*
> *Could know me too*
>
> *I'm old enough to be young*
> *And young enough to be me*
>
> *Yes, I am growing younger, it's true*
> *And as I do*
> *I want to know you*

It was up to me to put it all together—rent a piano, circulate flyers, and put ads in the trade papers. It was worth all the effort. The show ran at the Olive Tree twice every weekend from late June through late October 1970. Ruth Young and another good pianist Edith Hillman took turns as music director from one weekend to the next. Some of the performers from earlier productions also performed on alternate weekends. As I would sit there in the café sipping coffee and watching the show, I could tell that it was working really well and that the children and the adults who had brought them were all enjoying it very much.

A review in the paper *Show Business* described the show as "a freestyle children's musical which radiates the child from within." The same review said the lyrics, dialog, and music "have a sort of Christopher Robin charm.

"

21

Keeping Up With the Times

In the early 1970s, I was still enrolled in the Herbert Bergoff Studio Workshop, Writing for the Musical Theater, and writing most of my music to the meaningful and imaginative words of Roberta Kassan. One of our shows, A *Shower of Gold*, was based on a short story by *New Yorker* writer Donald Barthleme. Mr. Barthleme, however, refused to give us permission after the fact to make a musical adaptation of his story. We were not "name" writers. So how could he know if the adaptation had any lyrical or musical value, I remember thinking sardonically.

Even though this was a workshop on writing for the musical theater, Bobbie Kassan and I did try our hands at a few individual songs in an effort to keep up with the changing musical times. Neither of us really liked what was happening musically or lyrically, yet, paradoxically, in trying to write in the new idioms we did open ourselves up a little. Here is one of our efforts. It has a modified rock underpinning.

Tryin' To Find The Beat
(© 1976)

Sometimes I think I know the answer,
Like a dancer I feel the beat.
Sometimes I think I've made my life complete, but
Sometimes the answer doesn't reach me,
Doesn't teach me what life is for.
Sometimes I think there must be something more.

People used to know how their life should go.
Were they only acting, was it all for show? Tell me

What can we do but look for answers
Like those dancers up on their feet?
What can we do but hope for music
And try to find the beat?

Actually, I had little more understanding of or appreciation for the folk music and protest songs of the day than I had for rock and roll. "After all," I said to myself, "a song is not a sociological tract." Still, in order to be "with it," I wrote some of them too, both with Roberta Kassan and with others. Here is a folk type song written with Sandra Lamont, another co-writer I was glad I knew.

The Singer Of Songs
(© 1963, © renewed 1991)

Verse 1

He told me that he was a traveling man,
The singing of songs was his trade.
He'd stay for a week or a month in a town,
And wherever they let him he played.

Chorus

I've been to mobile,
I've been to Saint Jo,

I've traveled from Frisco to Chi,
I carry my songs wherever I go;
I'll be singing my songs 'til I die.

Verse 2

He told me that he was a wandering soul,
That bread and a bed were his pay.
And wherever he found there was mis'ry or shame
Well, he'd stop for a while and he'd play.

Verse 3

He told me he'd heard that in Birmingham town
While black men were kneeling to pray
That four of their children were killed by a bomb,
So he went there to sing and to play.
(repeat chorus)

Verse 4

They put him in jail down in Birmingham town.
They told him it wasn't his fight.
The black men were giving them trouble they said
And they wanted their town to be white.

Verse 5

That wasn't the end of his travelin' days—
He's leaving for Georgia today.
And whenever he hears that a man needs a song
Then he'll stop for a while and he'll play.
(repeat chorus)

The feeling that I owed it to myself as a writer to make at least some effort to keep up with current musical trends stayed with me. So in late 1975, I enrolled in the songwriters workshop at the American Guild of Authors and Composers, now named the Songwriters Guild of America.

The workshop was conducted by two high school music teachers from the borough of Queens. Both of them had had some success in songwriting. Ted and Libby were very competent in the craft of songwriting, and both, being thoroughly conversant with all aspects of the music business, made excellent workshop moderators. Their critiques of our songwriting efforts were astute but were always made from the standpoint of what they considered to be commercial. Though both had come of age when popular music had a different quality than it now had, I felt that both were pretty much given over to rock and roll. I imagine that the unprecedented success of the Beatles was enough to convince them that there was more of value in their songs and records than I heard.

Of course, Ted and Libby had a point. If you're going to conduct a workshop on songwriting, it behooves you to be commercially oriented. They did not pretend that this was a scholarly musicological seminar.

Even so, the shortest distance between two points is hardly ever a straight line, and I, for one, needed to justify to myself the effort I was making by feeling that in learning to write in a contemporary idiom I was adding something to my musical resources. I wanted to integrate these new elements into my own style, rather than arbitrarily graft them on by slavishly imitating the latest hit song in my writing. And I believe that over time I did achieve such integration in some of the songs I wrote.

In fact, I wrote one such song with Ted and Libby themselves. It was called "One Step Ahead of the Blues." Ted showed me the lyric and asked me how I would set it musically. I thought it was quite good and original and worked hard until I ended up with what I considered to be the right musical setting for it. Libby then took one of my seminal musical ideas and developed it as she heard it. The result was very good and her version was settled on, but I was still given equal writing credits with the two of them.

I felt that this was a real step up for me. Imagine a student being asked by his teacher to help out with something. We had a good demonstration tape made of the song and Ted took it to a big record company executive he knew. This man announced that it was the best song he had heard in a year.

Maybe this would turn out to be the kind of break people are always talking about.

However, a couple of weeks later Ted took me aside after the workshop session. He wanted me to understand that the fact he had given me the lyric to work on didn't mean that he and Libby were asking me to write with them on any kind of permanent basis. Whether or not I had made that assumption I don't now remember. I probably had. But o.k., so be it. I had learned something in their workshop, and I could now add them to the list of people with whom I have written only one song.

22

Songwriting Get-Togethers

The happiest result of the songwriting workshop described in the last chapter was that in it I met several people with whom I would be writing for several years. While in the workshop, many of us had shown interest in and admiration for each other's work and so decided, when the formal workshop ended, to meet in a different friend's apartment each week and compare notes. No pun intended.

Some of us wrote mainly music, some lyrics, and we soon found ourselves pairing off with different members of the group for different songs. Our critiques of each other's work were honest and helpful.

All of the members of this group were younger than I, but we all had the same objective—to learn how to write successfully in the commercial market of the day—the mid-seventies—yet we all wanted to keep our individuality, musical and lyrical. The fact that they were younger than I and had not spent many years writing in the traditional pop music idiom was a great help in opening me up musically and lyrically. Yes, lyrically, because I was beginning to work with them on the lyrics of some of the songs we were writing together.

I will try to illustrate how my songwriting was evolving by showing the differences between one of the first songs I ever wrote and one that I wrote thirty years later with one of my workshop buddies.

"Somewhere by the Sea" was written in 1947 with my first lyric co-writer, William L. Hubbell. The music was written first and adhered to one of the strict musical forms of the day—a verse of twelve measures followed by a chorus in the form ABAC—each section being eight measures long. The words have a generalized and poetic quality and tell a little story.

Somewhere by the sea
(© 1946, © renewed 1974)

Verse

Though winter winds are blowing,
I hear the ocean sigh
And know I must be going
Out where the grey gulls cry;
And my heart and I together
Will remember the soft May weather.

Chorus

It was springtime one-time
Somewhere by the sea
I held heaven in my arms.

You and I built castles in the sand that day
Hoping that they would really stand some way.

Now the winter time is somehow in my heart
I must go where white caps toss.

Maybe I can find the love I lost that day
Waiting somewhere by the sea.

"We Never Even Danced" was written in 1976 with Janet Cohen. The words were written first and are in the much-used storytelling form: Verse-Chorus, each sixteen measures long. There is a second verse with different words, but the chorus is repeated as is.

We Never Even Danced
(© 1976)

Verse 1

We did things people do when they're falling in love—
We made plans, didn't leave much to chance.
I learned to laugh and lean a little on you,
But we never even danced.

Chorus 1

We never even danced.
Your arms didn't stay around me that long.
You left me before we could even choose our own love song.
We never even danced;
And though you spent many nights in my bed,
We left way too much unsaid.

Verse 2

I thought you and I had a future in mind,
Thought we'd both give our feelings a chance;
But you walked out before I got to know you,
And we never even danced.

Chorus 2

We never even danced.
Your arms didn't stay around me that long.
You left me before we could even choose our own love song.
We never even danced;

How could love that felt so right go so wrong?
No, we never even danced.

I like to think that my music is right for this newer, more flexible form, but that it still has a quality I hope is distinctive.

23

Finding the Music Inherent in the Words

*F*rom 1946, when I wrote my first song, until 1955, when I was staff composer at White Roe Lake resort in the Catskills, I wrote entire thirty-two-measure melodies to songs before giving them to a lyric co-writer for words. At White Roe Lake, I began writing music to words already written by entertainment director, Richard Diamond.

When I returned to New York and began writing with Chandler Warren, I had more practice in setting music to words already written. First, there were the two Columbia University Law School revues—1956 and 1957. Then in 1958 came our musical adaptation of *Alice in Wonderland* written in collaboration with Dorothy Love. This show had a successful run at the Orpheum Theatre on Second Avenue.

Already, a writing modus operandi was becoming apparent. Whether I was writing with someone from the same locale or writing with Chandler Warren in Los Angeles when he opened his entertainment law firm there, I would always give my co-writer a complete song melody or he or she would give me a complete lyric. Only on very rare occasions have I sat with a co-writer and puzzled out one lyrical or musical phrase at a time. I am not suggesting that one way of writing is better than another. I am only describing what my way of writing has been.

As to whether I preferred writing the music first or setting music to lyrics, my opinion and preference opened up as I wrote more. During the years that I always wrote the music first, I was convinced that for the greatest songs the music had been written first. I attempted to substantiate this all-knowing generalization by pointing out that Richard Rodgers wrote his best music with Lorenz Hart because in the team Rodgers and Hart, the music always came first. I went on to say that the songs by my favorite composer, Jerome Kern, more often than not had had the music written first.

All that was needed to make these pronouncements questionable was to examine some of the songs Rodgers wrote with Oscar Hammerstein and see how successful he was in setting these lyrics to beautiful music. It has often been pointed out that in the musical theater works of Rodgers and Hammerstein the song lyrics became an integral part of the dialog and helped advance the action of the play. It is also true that when the words are written first, the old song forms, AABA and ABAC, with eight measures of music allotted to each letter, are more often than not expanded or changed altogether.

I would like to illustrate this kind of expansion and transformation with a song from a show I have written with another co-writer, Roberta Kassan. The name of the show is *Happy All the Time*. Its subject is life in a retirement community. The song "Even Here, Even Now" is sung by two of the leading characters near the end of the musical. I hope to show how Ms. Kassan has contracted and expanded the AABA song form in a way that in this instance makes it more interesting. I like to say that the music I wrote was inherent in her words and that it was just a question of my recognizing it.

Even Here, Even Now
(© 1990)

It can happen any time

A
Even here, even now, 6 measures
Don't you see?

Love can come at any age,

A
Even here, even now, 6 measures
Look at me!

I'm no one special, past my prime.
You restored me late in time,

B
Showed me I can feel again, 8 measures
Made me see I'm real again.

I'm Rip Van Winkle in reverse,
Wakened from a deadly curse,

B
Finding I can love again, 8 measures
Knowing I can live again.

It has happened just in time,

A
Even here, even now. 6 measures
Be with me.

Love has happened one last time
Even here, even now,

A
Stay with me, 6 measures
Stay with me.

Writing the music first to an AABA song it would be almost unthinkable to repeat the B section, the bridge, and to repeat the final A section. But here, the words in both those stanzas strengthen the song greatly.

24

Warren and Miles
(Individual Songs)

Ending chapter 16 with Chandler Warren's lyric to our song "Tell Me Softly" can serve as the first note in an account of our writing career together, which began in 1956 with the first Columbia Law School revue and is still going on. It is not surprising that I have written more individual songs and musical theater works with Chandler Warren than with any other writer whose work I have discussed in this autobiography.

Not long after the music manuscript of "Tell Me Softly" was circulated to singers Chandler Warren and I knew and liked, one of them, Marion Montgomery, a Mississippi friend of Chandler's, sang it in California venues and recorded it for her album "Sometimes in the Night," Prestige LP 532. She sang and recorded many other songs of ours as well, including "Point Me in the Right Direction," "All it Takes is a Little Time," "Who's Afraid of Tomorrow?" "Wish Me Luck," and "I Don't Cry Anymore," to name just a few.

It was not long after this that Marion rejoined her husband Laurie Holloway in England. Mr. Holloway, an orchestral arranger, arranged "Tell

Me Softly" for orchestra, and Marion sang it on the British Broadcasting Corporation, the famous BBC.

Chandler Warren and I and my wife, Jeanne, had our favorite cabaret singers and were, in fact, lucky enough to know some of them—the late Blossom Dearie for one. I am going to insert here an entry from my 1984 journal that I think is very much to the point:

Listening to Blossom last night I was concentrating on her left hand playing the bass line. This was remarkably right like everything else she does. What is so preeminently good about her performances is her sense of musical proportion. The songs are put in their proper setting, in the right frame. They are set off in the way that is just right for them. She knows just how long each musical interlude should be, just how long each musical postlude—when to sing, when not to sing. With Blossom the song never ends a second or a measure before it should or ever goes a syllable or a note too long. *Her* composition, which surrounds the other composition—the song—is entirely appropriate. The picture has been given the only frame that is right for it.

You can imagine, then, how delighted we all were when Blossom Dearie began singing "Tell Me Softly" in New York nightclubs and included it in her album "Positively Volume VII," Daffodil Records LP, 1983. She shared the vocal with an excellent male vocalist, Grady Tate. The bass player was Jay Leonhart, one of the best.

I can't leave "Tell Me Softly" without telling about the night another of our favorite cabaret singers, Steve Ross, sang it in Symphony Space, a former movie theater on upper Broadway in New York. I will never forget that, when Steve finished the song, a woman behind us let out a heavy gasp, an expression of disbelief. This impressed and pleased us more than the applause all around her.

We want to say "thanks" and pay tribute to another strong and engaging cabaret singer, Jane Scheckter, who, with strong piano backing by Don Rebic, has performed in New York venues quite a few Warren and Miles seminal songs, "One-Man Woman," "I Don't Cry Anymore,"

"Charity," and "But Love (That's Another Game)," to name just a few. As noted earlier, Jane played the part of one of the children in the musical, *Four O'Clock Children*.

But Love (That's Another Game)
(© 1989)

Mister Hoyle has written rules
For the games that people play.
Even simple-minded fools
Can follow what he has to say.
But there's one game of the heart
That Mister Hoyle has failed to chart.

I always win at Scrabble,
And at Bridge it is the same,
But love, love, love—
That's another game.

I always hit the target
For I have perfect aim,
But love, love, love—
That's another game.

Bad times elude me,
Guest lists include me,
I don't get caught in the rain.
but when I see you
I guarantee you
My heart can't take the strain.

I am the best at tennis
And at golf I've won some fame,
But love, love, love—
That's another game.

Love isn't scrabble,
Bridge or backgammon,

They're all just the same.
But love, love, love—
That's another game.
Love, love, love,
That's another game.

One of the most flattering things I ever experienced was when vocalist Janet Hariton and pianist and vocalist William Lewis recorded a CD entitled "Much Ado About Love–Songs by Harold Arlen and Robert Miles." Imagine sharing CD space with such classic American popular songs as "This Time the Dream's on Me" and "Happiness is Just a Thing Called Joe"? I still can't believe it.

One of the songs Chandler Warren and I were represented by on this CD was the touching, "How Do I Feel?" It shows that a lot can be said in a few words:

How Do I Feel?
(© 1988)

How do I feel when you tell me it's over
And I lie awake until dawn?

How do I feel when you say you don't love me,
That you just don't want to go on?

How do I feel when I reach for your hand,
Which you slowly, but surely withdraw?

How do I feel when the telephone rings
And it's you on the end of the line?

What do I say when you ask how I'm feeling?
"I'm just fine," I say, "thank you, I'm fine."

A few years later, Janet Hariton and William Lewis put together a cabaret show made up completely of Miles songs, written with different lyricists. Seven of these songs have lyrics by Chandler Warren. When recorded on CD, this program was given the title "Miles of Love, Journeys Through the Heart." A fitting way to end this chapter is with Mr. Warren's lyric to our song, "You Never Get Too Much Love."

You Never Get Too Much Love
(© 1990 by Warchan Music Co., ASCAP

You can drink too much liquor
Or take too many pills.
You can eat too much dinner
Or have too many thrills.
You can have too much coffee
Or all of the above,
But you never get too much love.

You can hear too much gossip
Or wear too many hats.
You can buy too much sugar
Or raise too many cats.
You can laugh till it hurts you
Or all of the above,
But you never get too much love.

You can oversleep and overwork
You better believe.
You can overtire on overtime
And overachieve.

You can eat too much pastry
Or climb too high a hill.
You can hear too much music
Or charge too large a bill.
You can smoke till it kills you
Or all of the above,
But you never get too much love.

Be overactive if you must
Or over-trusting with your trust,
But there's one thing there's not enough of.

You can do too much talking
And make too many starts.
You can spend too much money
Or play too many parts.
You can make too much whoopee
Or all of the above,
But you never get too much,
Not for a moment.
You never get too much love.

25

Warren and Miles
(Musical Theater Works)

As related earlier, the first musical theater works Mr. Warren and I wrote were the Columbia University Law School Revues in 1956 and 1957. It was a year later 1958 that Chandler presented me with a fanciful and engaging libretto to *Alice in Wonderland*. It was a real treat, a delight to find the right music inherent in songs like "The Maddest Tea Party," containing a lot of word play and "Wonderland is Just a Dream Away," with its flowing and expressive phrases. The show was first produced at the Orpheum Theatre in lower Manhattan. It was later put up by Opera on the Go in the borough of Queens as well as by theaters in other parts of the country.

Wonderland Is Just A Dream Away
(© 1964)

Would you like to meet your dreams someday?
It's easy for they're not so far away.
Just remember when you dream

Your dreams will all come true.
Suddenly you'll find a land so wonderful to you.

In your boat of stars you'll drift along
Where all the air is filled with love and song.
Then you'll wonder why the world
Can't be like this each day, for
Wonderland is just a dream away.

The Old Lady-Shows Her Medals is based on the play of the same name by Sir James M. Barrie. It is about London charwomen in World War I, one of whom "adopts" a soldier who is home on leave for a few days. This charwoman, Mrs. Dowey, expresses her feelings in song after Kenneth, the soldier, has returned to the front.

Isn't It Better?
(© 1983)

Isn't it better to have known him for a little while
Than never to have known him at all?
Isn't it better to have owned him for a moment's time
Than never to have owned him at all?

I know he won't be home for Christmas.
I'll get no card on Valentine's Day.
But I have him here, here in my heart,
And in my heart is where he'll always stay.

In 1999 this show was given a staged reading at the Stella Adler Theatre in Hollywood. The lead part of Mrs. Dowey was taken by Broadway actress, Charlotte Rae.

The Happy Prince is a one-act, fifty-minute musical based on a story by Oscar Wilde. It is about a statue who finds happiness by divesting himself of his bejeweled eyes and other priceless accoutrements in order to help the suffering and needy he can see from his lofty position in the village. One of the songs in this show says it all:

It's Better To Give
(© 2000)

It's better to give than to receive
I believe.
It's better to give than to receive.

Making someone happy
Will make you happy too.
When you do good for someone else
You're also doing good for you.

It's better to give than to receive
I believe.
It's better to give than to receive.

Giving someone pleasure
Will give you pleasure too.
Just make another person smile,
You'll find he's smiling just for you.

It's better to give than to receive
I believe.
It's better to give than to receive
I believe, I believe.
It's better to give than to receive.

Facing the Facts of Love is not a "book show," but a revue with many different and different kinds of songs performed by many different singers, both solo and in ensemble. This show has had several productions both Off-Broadway in New York and in Los Angeles. The rousing title song is sung by the whole company.

Facing The Facts Of Love
(© 1976)

It's great,
It's grand;
The whole situation is well in hand
'Cause you
And I
Are facing the facts of love.

It's real,
It's right;
The whole world looks rosy and bright tonight
'Cause you
And I
Are facing the facts of love.

Ev'ryone told us that love is a boomerang playing its tricks on you.
No matter how often that silly rumor rang
This time it didn't ring true.

It's new,
It's nice;
We're trapped in a wonderful paradise.
With no more strife
It's a laughable, lovable, livable life
Since you
And I
Are facing the facts of love.

The musical revue has room for the humorous and the regional. Consider the following male stanza from a duet:

You're Cuter Than A Kokopelli
(© 2012)

You're cuter than a Kokopelli
You're finer than the art in Taos.
You're sweeter than red pepper jelly.
You're warm as an adobe house.

You're quainter than a Zuni fetish.
You're tastier than blue corn meal.
Just like a burro you're coquettish.
I 'm sure that we could make a deal.

I'll be the salsa on your chip,
Or be your guacamole dip,
The margarita that you sip.
Can't you see how you've conquered me?

You're hotter than my mama's chile.
You are the saint in Santa Fe.
You're quicker than a new-born filly.
I love you, baby. Say you'll stay.

Fauntleroy is a musical version of the world-famous novel *Little Lord Fauntleroy*, by Frances Hodgson Burnett published in 1885. Chandler Warren's libretto and lyrics to this adaptation were a delight to set to music. It was given its world premier, complete with orchestra, in September 2009 at the Natchez Little Theatre, Natchez, Mississippi. The reception was enthusiastic. There have been several productions of the show at this theater since then, and more are scheduled.

Reviewing the show for *The Natchez Democrat*, James P. McCollum explains that Mr. Warren's libretto and lyrics have restored the "Little Lord" from the foppish stereotype he suffered under for many years to the healthy American kid who is able to transform his English grandfather from a heartless lord into a considerate and reasonable man.

An earlier article in the same paper had stated, "Miles' music is exquisite and pays homage to the great composers of Broadway from the earlier part of the 20th century. The tunes and lyrics are memorable, and the show is sure to delight audiences of all ages." McCollum concludes his review by stating, "These are songs that, should *Fauntleroy* go to Broadway, could become stage musical classics." Also, "If this work goes to Broadway, Warren may have created the most powerful child's role since Annie."

Here is what Cedric Errol's mother thinks of him:

Love's The Only Thing He Knows
(© 2009)

He doesn't have an evil thought
From his head down to his toes.
He's as happy as a lad could be
For love's the only thing he knows.

He's not the least bit cynical.
He's innocent as a lamb.
I don't mean to be clinical,
But he's trying to be
The way that he thinks I am.

To hate is far beyond his ken;
He's been sheltered I suppose.
Everyone he meets becomes his friend
For love's the only thing he knows.
Yes, love's the only thing he knows.

In addition to the full-length musical theater works just described, Chandler Warren and I have written a number of one-act, fifty-minute musicals suitable for productions in high schools with casts made up of students. *Nightingale*, for example, suggested by the Hans Christian Andersen's *The Emperor's Nightingale*, conveys the message that song has the power to lift one's spirits and thus to heal. The further truth is that only when free can one function properly. In this show the Nightingale cannot sing when caged. *Nightingale* was given a number of performances by students at the Totino-Grace High School in Edina, Minnesota.

Other Warren and Miles shows in this genre are *The Princess Who Couldn't Cry*, based on the opera *Turandot* by Puccini; *Rapunzel, Rich Brother, Poor Brother*, and *The Three Golden Hairs*, all based on stories by the Brothers Grimm. By no means to be overlooked is *The Snipe Hunt*, which is based on an original story by Mr. Warren himself.

Well, readers, that's it. Having now finished this autobiography, I can get back to writing music. In fact, Chandler Warren has just sent me one of his first-rate lyrics.

Goodbye and best wishes.

26

Music of Robert Miles

HOW DO I FEEL?

LYRIC BY: CHANDLER WARREN (ASCAP)   MUSIC BY: ROBERT MILES (ASCAP)

SLOW TO MEDIUM TEMPO

HOW DO I FEEL WHEN YOU TELL ME IT'S O-VER AND I LIE A-WAKE UN-TIL DAWN? HOW DO I FEEL WHEN YOU

SAY YOU DON'T LOVE ME, THAT YOU JUST DON'T WANT TO GO

ON? HOW DO I FEEL WHEN I

REACH FOR YOUR HAND, WHEN YOU SLOW — LY BUT SURELY WITH —

DRAW? HOW DO I FEEL WHEN THE

TEL-E-PHONE RINGS AND IT'S YOU ON THE END OF THE LINE?—

WHAT DO I SAY WHEN YOU ASK HOW I'M FEEL-ING? I'M JUS'

FINE," I SAY, "THANK YOU, I'M FINE."—

THE SINGER OF SONGS

WORDS BY: SANDRA LAMONT
MUSIC BY: ROBERT MILES-ASHE

SOMEWHERE BY THE SEA

LYRIC BY: WILLIAM HUBBELL

MUSIC BY:

VERSE - WITH EXPRESSION

THOUGH WINTER WINDS ARE BLOWING, I HEAR THE O—CEAN SIGH AND KNOW I MUST BE GO—ING OUT WHERE THE GREY GULLS CRY; AND MY HEART AND I TO—GETH—ER WILL RE-MEM-BER THE SOFT MAY WEATH-ER,

POCO RIT.

COPYRIGHT RENEWED 1974

CHORUS - MODERATELY AND EVENLY

IT WAS SPRINGTIME ONE-TIME SOMEWHERE BY THE SEA

I HELD HEAV-EN IN MY ARMS, YOU AND

I BUILT CAS-TLES IN THE SAND THAT DAY

HOP-ING THAT THEY WOULD REALLY STAND SOME-WAY.

NOW THE WIN-TER TIME IS SOME-HOW IN MY HEART

I MUST GO WHERE WHITE CAPS TOSS, MAY-BE

I CAN FIND THE LOVE I LOST THAT DAY

WAIT — ING SOME-WHERE BY THE SEA.

TRYIN' TO FIND THE BEAT

LYRIC BY: ROBERTA KASSAN (ASCAP)

MUSIC BY: ROBERT MILES (ASCAP)

MODERATE AND EASY

SOME-TIMES I THINK I KNOW THE AN-SWER. LIKE A DAN-CER

I FEEL THE BEAT. SOME-TIMES I THINK I'VE MADE MY LIFE COM-

PLETE. BUT SOME-TIMES THE AN-SWER

DOES-N'T REACH ME, DOES-N'T TEACH ME WHAT LIFE IS FOR.

SOME-TIMES I THINK THERE MUST BE SOME-THING MORE.

PEO-PLE USED TO KNOW — HOW THEIR LIFE SHOULD GO, —

WERE THEY ON-LY ACT-ING? WAS IT ALL FOR SHOW? TELL ME

WHAT CAN WE DO BUT LOOK FOR AN-SWERS LIKE THOSE DAN-CERS

UP ON THEIR FEET? WHAT CAN WE DO BUT HOPE FOR MU-SIC AND

TRY TO FIND THE BEAT?

TRY ————————— TO FIND THE BEAT?

TWENTY-ONE MILES FROM HOME

Words by
WILLIAM K. HUBBELL

Music by
ROBERT MILES, JR.

Verse

I wan-der'd in-to the coun-ty jail, one Sun-day af-ter-noon, And
in his cell a cow-boy sat sing-ing this un-hap-py tune:

Chorus

This lone-some heart of mine is a-was-tin', So close to my home, boy,
Just twen-ty-one miles. My moth-er's food I seem to be

tas - tin', Her blue-ber-ry pie, boy, Is sweet as her smiles.

I al-ways thought home was made just for sleep-in', But now it's

keep-in' my ver-y own soul. So home is

where this cow-boy is head-in', Just twen-ty - one miles when

I get my pa-role. role.

TWENTY-ONE MILES FROM HOME-2

WE NEVER EVEN DANCED

LYRIC BY: JANET COHEN

MUSIC BY: ROBERT MILES

1. WE DID THINGS PEO-PLE DO WHEN THEY'RE FALL-ING IN LOVE
2. I THOUGHT YOU AND I HAD A FU-TURE IN MIND,

WE MADE PLANS, DID-N'T LEAVE MUCH TO CHANCE;
THOUGHT WE'D BOTH GIVE OUR FEEL-INGS A CHANCE;

I LEARNED TO LAUGH AND LEAN A LIT-TLE
BUT YOU WALKED OUT BE-FORE I GOT TO

ON YOU, BUT WE NEV-ER E-VEN DANCED. WE NEV-ER
KNOW YOU AND WE NEV-ER E-VEN DANCED.

E-VEN DANCED. YOUR ARMS DID-N'T STAY A-ROUND ME THAT

LONG. YOU LEFT ME BE-FORE WE COULD E-VEN CHOOSE OUR OWN LOVE

SONG. WE NEV-ER E-VEN DANCED; AND THOUGH YOU SPENT

MAN-Y NIGHTS IN MY BED, WE LEFT WAY TOO MUCH UN-

SAID. HOW COULD LOVE THAT FELT SO RIGHT GO SO

WRONG? NO, WE NEV-ER E-VEN DANCED.

WORDS

LYRIC BY: CHANDLER WARREN (ASCAP)   MUSIC BY: ROBERT MILE (ASCAP)

CHORUS: MEDIUM TEMPO WITH A LILT.

WORDS TRY TO TELL THE OLD STORY.

WORDS TRY TO SING OF LOVE'S GLO-RY.

LOV-ING WORDS, TEN-DER WORDS TRY IT EV-'RY DAY.

SIM-PLE WORDS, FAN-CY WORDS—HOW MUCH CAN THEY SAY?

WORDS   TRY TO HELP MY LIPS   TEACH YOU.

WORDS   TRY TO HELP MY ARMS   REACH YOU;   BUT

EV-'RY WORD THAT I SAY   NEV-ER SEEMS TO DO,   FOR

3

WORDS JUST CAN'T TELL HOW I LOVE YOU.

YOU NEVER GET TOO MUCH LOVE

LYRIC BY: CHANDLER WARREN (ASCAP)   MUSIC BY: ROBERT MILES (ASCAP)

MEDIUM TEMPO, RHYTHMICALLY FREE

YOU CAN DRINK TOO MUCH LIQ-UOR OR TAKE TOO MAN-Y PILLS, YOU CAN

EAT TOO MUCH DIN-NER OR HAVE TOO MAN-Y THRILLS, YOU CAN

HAVE TOO MUCH COF-FEE, OR ALL OF THE A-BOVE; BUT YOU

NEV-ER GET TOO MUCH — LOVE. YOU CAN HEAR TOO MUCH GOSSIP OR

WEAR TOO MAN-Y HATS, YOU CAN BUY TOO MUCH SUG-AR OR

RAISE TOO MAN-Y CATS, YOU CAN LAUGH TILL IT HURTS YOU, OR

ALL OF THE A-BOVE, BUT YOU NEV-ER GET TOO MUCH —

LOVE. YOU CAN O-VER-SLEEP AND O-VER-WORK YOU

BET-TER BE-LIEVE, YOU CAN O-VER-TIRE ON O-VER-TIME AND O-VER-A-CHIEVE. YOU CAN EAT TOO MUCH PAS-TRY OR CLIMB TOO HIGH A HILL. YOU CAN HEAR TOO MUCH MU-SIC OR CHARGE TOO LARGE A BILL. YOU CAN SMOKE TILL IT KILLS YOU, OR ALL OF THE A-BOVE; BUT YOU NEV-ER GET TOO MUCH LOVE. BE O-VER-AC-TIVE IF YOU MUST OR O-VER-TRUST-ING WITH YOUR TRUST, BUT THERE'S ONE THING THERE'S NOT E-NOUGH OF. YOU CAN DO TOO MUCH TALK-ING AND MAKE TOO MAN-Y STARTS, YOU CAN SPEND TOO MUCH MON-E-Y OR PLAY TOO MAN-Y PARTS, YOU CAN MAKE TOO MUCH WHOOP-EE OR ALL OF THE A-BOVE; BUT YOU NEV-ER GET TOO MUCH, —

NOT FOR A MO-MENT. YOU NEV-ER GET TOO MUCH—

LOVE.

KING BRAND